D1045658

BAKING SODA
BONANZA

BAKING SODA BONANZA

Peter A. Ciullo

HarperPerennial

A Division of HarperCollins*Publishers*

HarperCollins books may be purchased for educational, business, or sales promotional use. For information please write: Special Markets Department, HarperCollins Publishers, Inc., 10 East 53rd Street, New York, NY 10022.

FIRST EDITION

Designed by Nancy Singer

Library of Congress Cataloging-in-Publication Data

Ciullo, Peter A., 1954–
    Baking soda bonanza / by Peter A. Ciullo.
        p.   cm.
    Includes bibliographical references and index.
    ISBN 0-06-095097-8
    1. House cleaning. 2. Sodium bicarbonate. 3. Home economics.
I. Title.
    TX324.C57   1995
    648'.5—dc20   95-72

97 98 99 ❖/RRD 20 19 18 17 16 15 14

*In memory of Josephine Ciullo, Ida DeCiampis,
and Alice Arcari, who brought dignity and love
to good food and a clean home.*

CONTENTS

ACKNOWLEDGMENTS

Thanks, above all, to my family—Claudia, Marissa, and Adam.

A special debt of gratitude is owed John Pote, for giving me the idea, and Jerry Reen, for sharing his historical perspective.

Many thanks, as well, for the help and advice of the Hoffman family, Chris Lemmond, Tom Whitney, Dr. Wayne Sorenson, Steve Lajoie, Dr. William Jensen, and Jennifer Griffin.

INTRODUCTION

FROM ACID STOMACH
TO ACID RAIN

A book about baking soda? Skeptics may say that baking soda is about as compelling a topic as club soda. It is, nevertheless, as uniquely American as Coney Island hot dogs or corn-on-the-cob. The use of baking soda in the refrigerator, or to clean everything from battery terminals to teeth, was not the invention of Madison Avenue. Nearly all of the popular uses of baking soda—a.k.a. sodium bicarbonate, bicarbonate of soda, bicarb, and soda—touted in the Helpful Hints columns were developed by American consumers over the past 150 years. Its general use in the kitchen and its eventual use in and around the entire house is a paradigm of American ingenuity and pioneer spirit. Here is a simple, cheap food ingredient for which the American people conceived some unusual, certainly unintended, but nonetheless ingenious folk uses.

No one knows who first thought of putting baking soda in the refrigerator to absorb odors. But it worked and was a common practice long before a major manufacturer, with no little skepticism, launched a costly program to discover just how effective it was. Generations of Americans have brushed their teeth with baking soda—some routinely, others when the toothpaste ran out. It wasn't minty and it wasn't sweet, but it worked.

Now baking soda is to toothpaste marketing of the nineties what fluoride was in the fifties.

In North America, the home uses of baking soda surpassed simply baking long ago. In the rest of the world, baking soda remains a kitchen oddity. Where available, it is used almost strictly as an antacid. Industrial uses, on the other hand, have proliferated globally. In addition to packaged foods, sodium bicarbonate is used in blood dialysis, animal feeds, fire extinguishers, textile processing, oil well drilling muds, carpet cleaners, foam rubber, denture cleaners, and paint strippers, among other things. True to its tradition as a safe and natural ingredient for a healthy home environment, baking soda's unique attributes are now being broadly applied to controlling toxic metals in drinking water, improving waste treatment processes, and reducing the acid in smokestack emissions.

Baking soda is a natural ingredient. As sodium bicarbonate, it is available in virtually endless supply. It occurs in the minerals trona and nahcolite, in briney lakes and in lake sediments. The bicarbonate content of the oceans plays a key role in stabilizing the carbon dioxide content of the earth's atmosphere. Likewise, sodium bicarbonate is essential to the functioning of the human body. It helps to maintain the proper acid/alkaline balance of blood. It is the major vehicle of carbon dioxide transport from body tissue to the lungs. It is a primary component of the duodenal fluid that neutralizes stomach contents before they enter the intestinal tract. Sodium bicarbonate is also a component of saliva, where it helps to reduce the attack of orally generated acids on tooth enamel.

Although it exists as an abundant natural resource, baking soda depends on sophisticated processing to meet the stringent standards of quality and purity mandated for most of its many uses. This type of beneficial amalgam of nature and technology is a worthy model for our times. In the current age of acute environmental and ecological awareness, when chemicals are suspect and natural is preferred, baking soda has managed to transcend the political as possibly the world's "greenest" chemical.

BAKING SODA
RISES

aking soda in America began, naturally enough, with baking. Its foothold in American homes was based on its use as a leavening agent.

THE PEARLASH EVOLUTION

The discovery of baking soda began with potash, a crude potassium carbonate extracted from wood ashes. American colonists learned how to purify potash into the pearlash (a more concentrated potassium carbonate) that became an important ingredient to their booming soap- and glass-making businesses. By the mid-eighteenth century, production of potash and pearlash had grown from a cottage industry to a major commercial enterprise. The colonies, with trees to burn, began exporting huge amounts of these carbonates to England's glass and soap factories.

It was during the 1760s that the use of pearlash in baking became popular. Bakers had been using tedious and difficult hand kneading as well as long-rising sourdough starters to leaven bread. Pearlash's high potassium carbonate content made it quite alkaline, so it was initially added as a natural counter to the sourness caused by the acids in sourdough. Bakers discovered, however, that besides sweetening the dough, pearlash accelerated its rising by liberating carbon dioxide gas bubbles as it reacted with the sourdough acids and baking heat. This ability of pearlash to create in minutes the leavening gases that required hours from the natural sourdough yeasts revolutionized baking.

The popularity of pearlash was fueled by two nearly concurrent developments in the United States. In 1796, Amelia Simmons published the first American cookbook, *American Cookery,* which featured several recipes requiring pearlash. At the same time, Oliver Evans was pioneering the fine grinding of wheat into lighter, airier flour. Almost at once, the home baker had pearlash, a growing body of instructions on how to use it, and finer, increasingly available flours.

THE SODA ASH REVOLUTION

Although pearlash remained the premier industrial carbonate in America well into the nineteenth century, the American Revolution convinced the governments and industries of western Europe that their rapidly expanding need of American carbonates was politically and economically unwise. There was precious little European woodland left to sacrifice to wood ash, and the only natural alternatives were the limited supplies of crude carbonates produced from the ashes of seaweeds and plants. The situation became so alarming that in 1783 the French Academy of Sciences offered a prize for the best process for converting common salt (sodium chloride) to soda ash (sodium carbonate). Nicolas LeBlanc won the prize in 1791 for his method of reacting salt, sulfuric acid, coal, and limestone. Soon soda ash plants proliferated in Europe. The now plentiful local supply of sodium carbonate replaced imported American potassium carbonates.

SALERATUS

The development of today's leavening bicarbonate from the industrial carbonates of yore took different routes in Europe and America. European chemists bubbled carbon dioxide gas through solutions of sodium carbonate to form the less alkaline sodium bicarbonate. This chemical was dubbed saleratus, meaning "aerated salt." Saleratus was adopted by the medical community as a safe and effective treatment for acid stomach. By the 1830s, America's home bakers had discovered that the sodium bicarbonate imported for medical use was a superior (albeit expensive) leavening alternative to pearlash or the American version of saleratus. It released its carbon dioxide quickly in recipes and was less prone to bitter aftertastes.

American saleratus, potassium bicarbonate, was first made by Nathan Read of Salem, Massachusetts, in 1788. He suspended lumps of pearlash over the carbon dioxide–rich fumes of fermenting molasses. The dry pearlash absorbed the carbon dioxide, converting its potassium carbonate to potassium bicarbonate. By the early nineteenth century, brewers and distillers were making saleratus as a sideline in much the same way by taking advantage of the carbon dioxide released from their fermentation vats. American saleratus was less expensive than the imported variety, but it was not as pure and did not leaven as dependably.

America's bakers were ready for a saleratus that would work as well as the imported sodium bicarbonate but be as cheap as the domestic alternative. Two American entrepreneurs—one a doctor and the other a salesman—accepted the challenge to provide the sodium bicarbonate that would in time become the baking soda found in nearly every home.

THE DETERMINED DOCTOR

As America discovered the advantages of saleratus over pearlash, Dr. Austin Church, a Yale graduate, started experimenting with a new way to make sodium bicarbonate. On the basis of promising work begun in his kitchen in Ithaca, New York, Dr. Church decided to trade his medical practice for the commercial production of saleratus. In 1834 he uprooted his wife and children and moved to Rochester.

The process Dr. Church perfected in his Rochester factory started with the meticulous purification of English soda ash. This refined sodium carbonate was then spread thinly over canvas-covered wooden frames stacked in a sealed room. For three weeks, this room was filled with hot gases containing carbon dioxide from coal-fired ovens. By this dry carbonation method, the purified sodium carbonate was entirely converted to food-grade sodium bicarbonate.

It is not surprising that Dr. Church, with a physician's training in chemistry, saw opportunity and financial security in the commercial manufacture of a pure sodium bicarbonate. His choice of Rochester was equally well reasoned. Following the opening of the Rochester and Lockport section of the Erie Canal in 1823, Rochester's proximity to the wheat fields of the Genessee Valley had propelled it to the status of leading flour milling center of the United States. When the Church family arrived in 1834, Rochester had just recently received its city charter, Genessee Valley flour had earned worldwide fame, and the Rochester mills were turning out more than 300,000 barrels per year. Dr. Church's intent was presumably to produce saleratus in bulk for sale to the flour mills' far-flung customers.

The bulk saleratus business allowed the Church family an adequate existence, but apparently not an especially prosperous one. After a brief return to doctoring in Oswego, in 1846 Dr. Church moved his family to New York City, where he and his entrepreneurial brother-in-law, John Dwight, founded John Dwight and Company.

DWIGHT'S SALERATUS

Dwight realized that the key to success, in addition to bulk sales to commercial bakers and drug companies, would be to build a consumer franchise by selling packages of saleratus through the retail trade. The busiest port of the nation proved itself an excellent headquarters; in their first year of operation, distinctively red-labeled DWIGHT'S SALERATUS was offered to New York's storekeepers in bags of one pound or less.

Within a few years, Dwight's Saleratus capitalized on its claims of superior quality and value. It captured the New York market, and started expanding into every inhabited part of the United States and eventually into

Canada. Its prime competition, especially in rural areas, came from the well established imported saleratus sold loose in kegs. But the distinctive red-wrapped bags of Dwight's Saleratus became the baker's choice. By 1850, the American housewife could purchase Dwight's Saleratus from the general store for 4¢ a pound—quite an improvement over the $1.25 a pound her mother had paid for the import in 1820.

Success, of course, bred competition as other manufacturers saw there was money to be made in tapping this new market for low-cost, high-quality domestic bicarbonate. The 1860s witnessed new brands from small firms like Philadelphia's Burgin & Sons to the mighty Pennsylvania Salt Manufacturing Company. The most effective competition to emerge from the 1860s, however, was from Dr. Austin Church.

ARM & HAMMER

In 1865, the sixty-six-year-old Dr. Church retired from John Dwight & Company, and two years later helped his sons, James and Elihu Church—both successful businessmen in their own right—found Church & Company. Recognizing there was sufficient need in the rapidly expanding United States to accommodate a competitor with quality equal to Dwight's Saleratus, they constructed a factory in Greenpoint, Brooklyn, devoted to the manufacture and sale of sodium bicarbonate.

James had been a partner in the Vulcan Spice Mills, a Brooklyn mustard and spice business, from which he acquired the Arm & Hammer logo. This symbol represented the arm of Vulcan, Roman god of fire and metalworking, with hammer raised. While perhaps better suited to the spice trade, this trademark was distinctively recognizable and soon intimately associated with what became the country's best-selling bicarb. Dwight's Saleratus eventually adopted a memorable trademark of its own, modeled on Lady Maud, a famous Jersey cow from the 1876 Philadelphia Centennial Exposition. Soon thereafter it became known as "Dwight's Soda," "Cow Brand," and in time simply "Cow Brand Soda." Cow Brand and Arm & Hammer Bicarbonate of Soda became the dominant products in the chemical leavening business, but the rivalry was friendly and mutually beneficial.

In 1896, fifty years after John Dwight first sold Austin Church's saleratus, and nearly thirty years after their business interests had diverged, their descendants reunited the two leading bicarb producers into the Church & Dwight Company. Church & Co. brought Arm & Hammer, the leading U.S. brand, to the merger, while John Dwight & Co. brought Cow Brand, the leading Canadian product. Although the two companies were now joined and the sodium bicarbonate came from a single source, the two brands were kept distinct to capitalize on the consumer loyalty each had earned over the years. This was rewarded with continued growth into the early decades of the twentieth century, when the term "baking soda" was first used. This name was most likely intended to differentiate pure sodium bicarbonate from the baking powders in which it was just one of several ingredients.

Cow Brand Baking Soda was phased out of the U.S. market after World War II, and in Canada in 1992, when it was finally discontinued in favor of Arm & Hammer.

BAKING AND BEYOND

The growth of baking soda into a household necessity during the second half of the nineteenth century was aided by the complex changes in a rapidly developing United States. Dwight's Saleratus was born at nearly the same time as the nationwide tax-supported public school system. A literate society invited the publication of more cookbooks. Baking recipes routinely required saleratus, and in 1860 Dwight's company started distributing free recipe booklets of its own. The 1860s also saw the spread of baking powders and yeast cake as convenient new leavening agents, but these were found suspect by the influential stalwarts of the U.S. health food movement of those days. The railroads became the backbone of the United States, transforming it into a world-class grain producer and fostering the rise of American-style mass merchandising. The full-service general store gave way to self-service neighborhood markets and finally to giant supermarkets. Packaging, trademarks, advertising, and distribution developed in such a way that companies like Dwight's and Church's, with distinctive packaging and staunch consumer loyalty, established themselves securely. Baking soda remained the preferred home leavener for nearly everything but bread into the twentieth century.

The versatility, low cost, and high quality of baking soda led consumers to discover a wide variety of uses beyond leavening. As baking in the home eventually declined, these folk uses of baking soda grew and filled the void, and have been lately supplemented by a variety of commercial and industrial applications. Some folk uses have even developed into amazing commercial successes, like the two examples that follow.

NOT JUST CHICKEN FEED

As the twentieth century closes, food companies, not individuals, use most of the baking soda produced for leavening, but food uses account for only 16 percent of all the sodium bicarbonate sold in North America. The major consumers of baking soda today are cattle, not people.

Diary cows are bred to be milk factories, with top producers easily exceeding twelve gallons per day. Genetics determines the maximum output possible, but energy input dictates actual results. Energy comes from food, which is broken down by bacteria in the rumen (the partially digested food) and ultimately converted to milk. The digesting bacteria function at peak efficiency when the rumen is just slightly acidic.

Diary cows eat a range of feeds, from low energy, high fiber food like dry hay and dry grass, to high energy grains. Maximum milk production and milk fat content depend on a substantial level of the high energy grain in the cow's diet. But high grain, low fiber feeds require less chewing, which decreases saliva production. Since saliva contains naturally occurring sodium bicarbonate, less chewing makes the rumen more acidic. The more acidic the rumen, the less efficient its digesting bacteria become. When the bacteria become seriously inhibited, digestion slows, feed intake decreases, and milk production drops. Acid stomach in cows is corrected by supplementing the sodium bicarbonate in each cow's saliva with baking soda, which is blended right into the feed. This balances rumen acidity and maintains optimum output of milk.

A similar situation exists with beef cattle. To prepare for market, they eat a high energy, low fiber diet to maximize weight gain. Since this gain can exceed 100 pounds per month and the rancher is paid per pound, the efficiency of food conversion is very important. Like the dairy cow, the steer produces less bicarbonate-containing saliva with the easier-to-chew grain. As his rumen becomes more acidic, feed intake, feed efficiency, and weight gain drop. Sodium bicarbonate in the feed prevents this, allowing the steer to gain weight faster and be ready for market sooner.

The success of sodium bicarbonate supplementation of high energy cattle feed has made this its single largest use in North America. This success has also attracted the attention of other livestock breeders, who are adopting the use of sodium bicarbonate to maximize the health and economic value of their animals. And baking soda is not limited to improving our meat and milk supply. In chicken feeds, baking soda promotes tougher eggshells, so that breakage between the henhouse and your house is minimized.

DENTAL CARE

Sodium bicarbonate is the only product in use today that was on the original list of products accepted by the American Dental Association in 1931. It cleans and polishes, of course, but in the process it also reduces plaque and tartar buildup, deodorizes the mouth, and makes teeth feel clean. Until recently, its popularity was hampered by the inconvenient powder form, salty taste, and lack of cavity-fighting fluoride. Church and Dwight, the Arm & Hammer baking soda experts, corrected this in 1988 by marketing a minty baking soda toothpaste with fluoride. Their nationwide campaign proved so successful that today, baking soda toothpastes are offered by every major toothpaste producer and many smaller ones.

After six generations of baking soda's safe and effective use in dental care, scientists proved what Grandma knew all along. Baking soda is safe and nonirritating to all oral tissues—less than startling news for a natural component of saliva. Baking soda reduces stains and plaque by its gentle polishing action. Tests have shown that toothpastes with high levels (60 to 65 percent) of baking soda clean as well as toothpastes with conventional abrasives, while showing much less abrasion. The mild alkalinity of baking soda can also react with and remove substances that dull or stain teeth. More importantly, baking soda reduces decay by neutralizing plaque acids. By controlling plaque, it controls tartar. Scientists have even documented the ability of the leading baking soda toothpaste to eliminate bad breath from subjects fed cheeseburgers with onion and garlic. Not content that all bases were covered, they followed it up with a study conducted on subjects who each drank a can of warm beer and then smoked two unfiltered cigarettes. Baking soda prevailed.

HOME CARE

Cattle feed and toothpastes are just two of the applications of baking soda that originated with folk remedies. We can thank the many generations of clever and inventive bicarb boosters for the 100 or so folk uses that follow as well. They have provided valuable, safe, and effective alternatives to commercial chemical formulas in and around our homes.

THE HOUSEHOLD
ALTERNATIVE

The blend of American ingenuity and Yankee frugality during the first century or so of its commercial existence produced an incredible range of uses for baking soda around the home. Baking soda was, above all, a pure and inexpensive staple and an old standby for baking. Until fairly recently, "make do" was the ethic spurring application of baking soda to tasks undreamed of by Austin Church and John Dwight. There may have been a name brand scouring powder, tooth powder, kitchen cleaner, or mouthwash at the local grocery store, but the clever and thrifty homemaker could make do with the ever reliable baking soda. More often than not, making do provided fine results. And, in true American fashion, making do was seen as an emblem of resourcefulness rather than a reflection of low economic status. Homemakers started writing to the bicarb producers, and later to newspaper and magazine columnists with their latest brainstorms on how to use baking soda for nearly everything but baking.

In the past two decades, environmental concerns have caused a shift in focus for baking soda use. The smart and economical alternative to scores of specialized powders and potions for home and personal care has become the safe and natural alternative as well. Baking soda's versatility, purity, safety, and simplicity have recommended it to those who prefer to avoid organic solvents, harsh chemicals, and suspicious chemical additives in the products used in their homes.

Home use continues to grow because regardless of the user's motivation, baking soda is effective. It's used because it works. In spite of the fact that virtually all of the folk uses of baking soda were, by definition, developed and promulgated by users in the home, there are sound scientific reasons why baking soda is so effective in so many different applications.

BAKING SODA BUFFERS

The basis of most of baking soda's uses is its fundamental chemical nature. Even though a baking soda solution is weakly basic (slightly alkaline), it acts as a chemical buffer when acids or bases are added. It helps to bring them to its own nearly neutral state. In this way, baking soda can act as either an acid or base itself. In the presence of acids it acts as a neutralizing base. In the presence of bases it acts as a neutralizing acid. This dual nature accounts for many of baking soda's uses. Unquestionably, the most important use to which we all put the buffering properties of baking soda is the one we are born with—the bicarbonate ion is the naturally occurring component of blood that maintains its delicate acid/base balance.

BAKING SODA CLEANS

Baking soda is a triple threat cleaner, supplying detergency, gentle abrasion, and effervescence. Its mildly alkaline (basic) nature is the basis of its gentle cleansing action. Most dirt and grease contain fatty acids, which react with baking soda to form a soap. This soap, in turn, works to remove the rest of the dirt or grease components. While stronger alkalis, like lye or lye-based products, can produce more cleaning power, they are generally toxic or irritating, and not nearly as safe as baking soda on soiled surfaces or the user's hands.

Baking soda provides gentle abrasion in paste form, or dry on a damp sponge or toothbrush. The dissolved portion provides detergency for the soil lifted by the soft undissolved crystals. These crystals are softer than nearly any surface and break down readily in use, actually providing more polishing than abrasion. Baking soda cannot scratch most household surfaces, and can be added to soaps and detergents in the home to enhance their cleaning power. Besides reacting with soils to form cleansing soaps and physically lifting soil particles by gentle abrasion, baking soda can produce effervescent bubbles to lift dirt from most surfaces. All that's needed is baking soda, water, and a common kitchen acid like vinegar.

Baking soda's unique combination of cleaning effects has made it the safe cleaning alternative around the home for nearly everything from stained kitchen sinks, to mildewed shower tile, to teeth.

BAKING SODA DEODORIZES

Most deodorizers work either as a perfume (like a room deodorizer) to mask odors or an absorbent (like charcoal or coffee grounds) to physically entrap odors. Perfumes do not eliminate unpleasant odors; they just overpower them with a more acceptable scent. Absorbents eventually come to equilibrium with the air and release some of the odor originally contained. Baking soda neutralizes odors in the air. Many objectionable odors are either strongly acidic or strongly basic. Baking soda deodorizes by chemically reacting with acidic odors, like sour milk, or basic odors, like spoiled fish, and irreversibly converting them to a cleaner state.

Baking soda works best in a confined and somewhat humid space, such as a refrigerator, car trunk, or closet. Its deodorizing efficiency depends on how much odor it has to deal with and how long it has to work. The longer air is in contact with baking soda, the more odor neutralization takes place. In the refrigerator, an open box of baking soda will be effective for about three months.

Baking soda deodorizes in solution much as it does in the air. Solutions used as a mouthwash, a cutting board cleaner, or a hand cleaner will neutralize, for example, acidic onion and garlic odors and basic fish odors.

BAKING SODA EXTINGUISHES FIRES

In the presence of high heat, baking soda decomposes to sodium carbonate (soda ash), water, and carbon dioxide. It can be used on electrical fires in equipment and wiring, and flammable liquid fires involving grease, gasoline, oils, and solvents. It is not recommended for fires involving ordinary combustibles, like paper, cloth, wood, and plastics because they can reignite. Water is the most effective extinguisher for these. Commercial dry chemical, foam, and soda/water fire extinguishers all contain baking soda.

BAKING SODA WORKS

Baking soda is used most often in one of three basic forms: dry—sprinkled baking soda straight from the box, as a paste—three parts baking soda combined with one part water, or as a solution—four tablespoons baking soda dissolved in one quart of water.

The recipes that follow call for baking soda in one or more of these forms as well as in variations combining baking soda with other household ingredients.

These recipes are believed safe for their intended uses, but use your common sense. If there is any question about the colorfastness or delicacy of a soiled surface, try the formula on a small, inconspicuous part first. Use every ingredient, even everyday kitchen items like salt and vinegar, carefully to avoid irritation to eyes and skin. (When cleaning with any composition, whether as innocuous as baking soda or aggressive as a heavy-duty commercial toilet bowl cleaner, it is good practice to wear skin and eye protection.) Keep all chemicals out of the reach of children.

Test personal care formulas on a small patch of skin—the inside of the forearm, for instance—if you are concerned about sensitization or allergic reaction. Sterilize or at least meticulously wash all containers and mixing equipment for storing personal care formulas, especially those used near the eyes. If you have any reservations about using a formula in the eyes or on broken skin, seek the advice of a health care professional.

BAKING SODA IN THE KITCHEN

FRUIT CLEANER

Many people are concerned about the contents of the residues left on fruits like apples and pears. Clean fruit with a paste of three parts baking soda per one part water. For very waxy coatings add a few drops of gentle dishwashing liquid or liquid soap. Rinse well and dry.

RUBBER GLOVE LUBRICANT

It's good practice to wear rubber gloves for chores using any type of chemical cleaners or polishes. If you have trouble sliding your hands into the gloves, sprinkle a little baking soda into the fingers to ease the way.

DRAIN CLEANERS

Kitchen drains collect grease and other organic matter. When clogged, they must be opened by breaking up and dissolving the gunk with caustic lye or lye-based products. Avoid clogs by periodically cleaning drains with baking soda alone or in combination with salt and common cooking acids. Here are three recipes, in order of increasing strength, for keeping your drains clean.

DRAIN CLEANER I

2 cups baking soda
2 cups salt

Blend well and store in an airtight container. Periodically pour 1 cup of the mixture down the drain followed by 1 quart of boiling water. Allow to sit for several hours or overnight, then flush with hot tap water for 1 minute.

DRAIN CLEANER II

Cream of tartar is a mild acid. It reacts with baking soda to clean with effervescent action.

2 cups baking soda
2 cups salt
½ cup cream of tartar

Blend well and store in an airtight container. Periodically pour ¼ cup of the mixture down the drain followed by 1 cup of boiling water. Allow to sit for about 5 minutes, then flush with hot tap water for 1 minute.

DRAIN CLEANER III

½ cup baking soda
½ cup white vinegar

Pour the baking soda down the drain followed by the vinegar. Let sit for about 2 hours; be careful in case the bubbling action causes splashing. Flush with hot tap water for 1 minute.

SCOURING POWDERS

Baking soda on a damp sponge will tackle many jobs as well as abrasive commercial scouring powders and is among the most gentle cleaners for stains in colored porcelain sinks. For tougher jobs, you can blend the following ahead of time and have them ready when needed.

GENTLE SCOURING POWDER

1 cup baking soda
1 cup salt

Blend well and store in a covered container.

TOUGH SCOURING POWDER

Washing soda is sodium carbonate. You can find it with the laundry powders in the supermarket.

1 cup baking soda
¼ cup washing soda

Blend well and store in a covered container.

TOUGHEST SCOURING POWDER

The natural pumice or chalk abrasive makes this suitable for heavy-duty jobs. Take care to avoid scratching.

1 cup baking soda
1 cup borax
1 cup finely powdered pumice or chalk

Blend well and store in a covered container.

SCOURING LIQUIDS

Creamy liquid cleansers have become a popular alternative to powdered cleansers. Make your own liquid cleanser by mixing ¼ cup of baking soda with enough gentle dishwashing liquid to make a creamy lotion. Pour this into a clean plastic squeeze bottle and it's ready to use. For extra scouring power, add ¼ cup of finely powdered chalk.

FOOD CONTAINER DEODORANT

Glass and plastic storage containers for food and beverages sometimes absorb odors from their contents. Eliminate these odors by washing the container well, adding two tablespoons of baking soda, and filling with hot water. Shake well to dissolve the baking soda. Cover the container and allow it to soak for a couple of hours. Soak overnight for especially strong odors. Wash the container. Use this deodorizing treatment for milk and juice pitchers, thermal bottles, picnic jugs, ice chests, lunch boxes, ice buckets, ice cube trays, crisper boxes, and any other glass or plastic food container.

When storing seasonal items like picnic jugs and ice chests, add ½ cup baking soda before closing to keep them smelling fresh.

COFFEEPOT CLEANER

Wash glass and stainless steel coffeepots with a solution of four tablespoons of baking soda in one quart of water. For badly stained pots, scrub with a paste of three parts baking soda per one part water or soak for one hour in a solution of four tablespoons baking soda per quart of hot water. **Aluminum coffee or cooking pots should not be washed with any hot alkaline substance, including hot baking soda solution, because it will discolor or pit this metal.**

COFFEE MAKER CLEANER

Remove the aluminum filter basket if you have one and fill the reservoir with a solution of four tablespoons baking soda per quart of water. Run the coffee maker through one cycle. Repeat with two additional cycles of plain water. Clean exterior plastic surfaces as well with a baking soda solution or baking soda sprinkled on a damp sponge.

BURNT-ON FOOD SOFTENER

Food stuck or burned onto pots, pans, and casseroles of all compositions **except aluminum** can be softened for easy removal by covering the soiled surface liberally with baking soda. Add enough hot or boiling water to cover and let soak for about ten minutes, longer for stubborn soils. For especially tough messes, boil a solution of one tablespoon baking soda per cup of water in the cookware. After the burnt residue is softened, remove it with baking soda on a dampened nylon scrubber.

COOKING SPRAY CLEANUP

Cooking sprays provide the oily film that keeps food from sticking to bakeware. Where they are not covered by food when used, they can create a stuck-on skin of their own. Release this residue from glass, ceramic, and metal (except aluminum) bakeware using the same techniques described above for burnt-on food.

NONSTICK COOKWARE CLEANER

Nonstick cookware is popular, among other reasons, for being notoriously easy to keep clean. Nevertheless, if not cleaned thoroughly, buildup of grease and oil will leave stains that will reduce the coating's effectiveness. The following treatment is simple and effective.

NONSTICK COOKWARE CLEANER

2 tablespoons baking soda
½ cup white vinegar
1 cup water

Add the ingredients to the cookware, place on the stove, and boil for 10 minutes. Use the stove hood fan, open a window, or otherwise maintain adequate ventilation to minimize exposure to vinegar fumes. Wash as usual.

COFFEE/TEA STAIN REMOVER

Coffee and tea stains can be removed from plastic cups and dishes, china, cutting boards, butcher-block, and plastic laminate countertops by sprinkling on baking soda and scouring with a damp sponge. (This will also work for light burns on china and butcher block.) For especially tough stains on plastic laminate, cover with lemon juice, let soak for 45 minutes, then sprinkle on baking soda and rub with a damp sponge. Rinse well.

OVEN CLEANER

Lye-based oven cleaners are perhaps the most dangerous household cleaning chemicals. Clean a standard oven (**not** self-cleaning or continuous clean) when cold with a paste of three parts baking soda per one part water, a nylon scrubber, and plenty of elbow grease. For particularly tough stains, use equal parts baking soda and salt in the paste. In electric ovens, be careful not to get any type of chemical, whether commercial cleaner, baking soda, or salt, on the heating elements because they may corrode when heated and short out.

STOVETOP PARTS AND SURFACE CLEANERS

To clean burnt-on spills, boil enamel and stainless steel burner catch pans in a nonaluminum pan for a few minutes in a solution of one tablespoon baking soda per quart of water. This works for the cast-iron burners on gas stoves too. Grease and burnt-on food can be cleaned from stovetops with baking soda sprinkled on a damp sponge.

MICROWAVE OVEN CLEANER

If your microwave is overdue for a good cleaning, mix two tablespoons of baking soda into one cup of water in a one-quart microwave-safe bowl. Let this solution boil in the microwave on high for a few minutes so that the steam condenses on the inside walls. Wipe off the walls, the inside of the door, and the door seal with paper towels followed by a damp cloth or sponge.

WHITE APPLIANCE AND SINK BLEACH

When white enameled metal appliances or white porcelain sinks start to yellow try the following recipe. This contains bleach so be careful that it does not come into contact with paper, cloth, vinyl, pets, or children and that you use gloves and proper ventilation. **Do not use this on colored appliances or colored sinks.**

WHITE APPLIANCE AND SINK BLEACH

¼ *cup baking soda*
½ *cup bleach*
1 *quart warm water*

Mix together well. Apply with a sponge, let set for about 10 minutes, rinse well, and dry.

APPLIANCE CLEANERS/DEODORIZERS

Remove the top from a box of baking soda and place it on a refrigerator shelf. Replace it every three months. Pour the expired box in the garbage to deodorize or down the drain or garbage disposal to clean and remove odors.

Sprinkle some baking soda on the bottom of the automatic dishwasher to control odors between washes.

To remove stains, films, and odors from the insides of refrigerators, freezers, and automatic dishwashers use a scour of baking soda on a damp sponge, rinse well, and dry.

To keep the door gaskets on refrigerators, freezers, and automatic dishwashers clean and mildew-free, wash once a month with a solution of four tablespoons baking soda per quart of water.

DRIP TRAY CLEANER

There is a slide-out tray under most refrigerators to catch

water from the auto-defrost cycle. In theory, the heat generated by the refrigerator motor helps this water evaporate quickly. That's why the drip tray doesn't usually overflow and why most people ignore it. However, the water doesn't always evaporate quickly enough to prevent the growth of mold in this warm, moist environment. Scour drip trays periodically with baking soda on a damp sponge or nylon scrubber. For extra cleaning power, use equal parts baking soda and borax. After scrubbing, rinse well and dry.

LIQUID DISHWASHING DETERGENT BOOSTER

Some liquid detergents for hand dishwashing don't remove grease well. To improve their effectiveness, add two tablespoons of baking soda to the hot water in the dishpan along with the detergent. For particularly tough stuck-on food, sprinkle baking soda on the area and scour with a nylon scrubber.

KITCHEN GREASE REMOVER

Remove grease spots from painted (enamel) cabinets, stovetops, and stove backsplashes.

GREASE CUTTER

¼ cup baking soda
½ cup white vinegar
1 cup ammonia
1 gallon hot water

Mix the ingredients well. Wash the cabinets with the

cleaner and a sponge, rinse with clear water, and dry well. Use rubber gloves and maintain adequate ventilation. For painted surfaces, try on a small area first to ensure that the cleaner will not discolor the paint; this is intended for glossy enamel painted surfaces and might attack normal flat interior paint. For stubborn spots on stovetops and backsplashes use the same procedure with a nylon scrubber.

METAL LEGS CLEANER
The metal legs of kitchen chairs and tables can accumulate dirt, grease, and dried-on foods. These can be removed with baking soda sprinkled on a damp sponge or nylon scrubber. More resistant soils can be removed with a paste of three parts baking soda to one part water. Add a few drops of gentle dishwashing liquid if desired. Rinse well and dry.

VINYL SEAT CLEANER
Clean the vinyl seats and backs of kitchen chairs safely with baking soda sprinkled on a damp sponge. Rinse well and dry.

CLOTH SEAT CLEANER
Before using any cleaning preparation on cloth upholstery, check for colorfastness in an inconspicuous area.

Fresh oily or greasy food stains on cloth chair seats and backs can be absorbed with equal parts baking soda and salt. Sprinkle the powder on the stain, rub it lightly, leave for a few hours, then vacuum. These stains can also be cleaned with a paste of three parts baking soda per one part water. Rub the paste into the stain, let dry, and then brush or vacuum away.

TABLETOP CLEANER
Clean stains on glass or plastic laminate tabletops with baking soda sprinkled on a damp sponge or with a paste of three parts baking soda per one part water. Rinse well and dry.

TABLE SEAM CLEANER
If your laminate-top kitchen table separates to accept an extension piece, the seam between each piece may collect the dried-up residue of food and cleaners. When it's time to clean the seam, scour with a paste of three parts baking soda to one part water on a nylon scrubber. Rinse with a damp sponge and dry.

BABY HIGH CHAIR CLEANER
Avoid exposing baby's skin to harsh chemical residues. Clean and deodorize baby's high chair after every feeding with a solution of four tablespoons baking soda per quart of water. Scrub dried-on accumulations around tray rails, chair spindles, etc. with baking soda on a damp sponge or nylon scrubber.

SPONGE/SCRUBBER CLEANER
To renew and deodorize soiled kitchen sponges, nylon scrubbers, and scrub brushes, soak them overnight in a solution of four tablespoons baking soda per quart of water.

*   *   *

CUTTING BOARD DEODORIZER

Wood and butcher-block breadboards and cutting boards that have picked up fish, onion, or garlic odors can be deodorized by scrubbing with a paste of three parts baking soda per one part water followed by thorough rinsing and drying. For strong odors, leave the paste on for about ten minutes before rinsing.

HAND DEODORIZER

Neutralize onion, garlic, and fish scents on your hands by wetting them, sprinkling on baking soda, rubbing well, then rinsing and drying.

HEEL MARK REMOVER

Remove black heel marks on kitchen linoleum or vinyl flooring with baking soda on a damp sponge or nylon scrubber.

GARBAGE DISPOSAL CLEANER

With warm tap water running, turn on the disposal and pour in one cup of baking soda. Run the water until one minute after all the baking soda is gone. A periodic cleaning like this will keep the grinding mechanism grease-free.

BAKING SODA IN THE BATHROOM

HARD SURFACE CLEANERS

Virtually any hard surface in the bathroom can be cleaned with baking soda instead of solvent or caustic-based commercial preparations. For routine cleaning of plastic laminate countertops and backsplashes, ceramic tile, porcelain or fiberglass sinks, tubs, and showers, chrome fixtures, glass shower doors and mirrors, just scrub with baking soda on a damp sponge, rinse well, and dry. Baking soda is one of the safest "abrasives" on fiberglass. For tough stains on bathroom surfaces, cover with lemon juice and let soak for about thirty minutes, then scrub with baking soda on a damp sponge, rinse well, and dry. If the tile or fiberglass walls of your tub/shower enclosure have a heavy soap scum film, try the following:

DOUBLE DUTY SOAP SCUM CLEANER

¼ cup baking soda
½ cup white vinegar
1 cup ammonia
1 gallon warm water

Mix the ingredients well. Wearing rubber gloves and maintaining adequate ventilation, use a sponge mop to apply the solution liberally to the filmy walls. Rinse well.

SHOWER CURTAIN CLEANERS

Spot clean the mildew on shower curtains with baking soda on a damp sponge, nylon scrubber, or scrub brush.

If your plastic shower curtain is machine washable, fill the washing machine with warm water, then add ½ cup laundry detergent, ½ cup baking soda, two bath towels (they provide scrubbing action), and the shower curtain. Run through the entire wash cycle, then add 1 cup of white vinegar to the rinse water. Do not rinse out the vinegar or spin dry. Remove the curtain from the machine and hang immediately to air dry. As the curtain dries the wrinkles will disappear.

TILE/GROUT STAIN REMOVERS

A simple baking soda paste made from three parts baking soda per one part water attacks rust stains on ceramic tile and mildew stains on grout. Use a nylon scrubber on tiles and an old toothbrush on grout. For especially tough stains, substitute household bleach for water. Wear rubber gloves and maintain adequate ventilation while you work. Rinse thoroughly.

TOILET BOWL CLEANERS

Instead of using bleach, acid, or lye-based cleaners in your toilet bowl, clean routinely with baking soda and a toilet brush. For stained bowls, pour in ½ cup baking soda and ½ cup vinegar and scrub with a toilet brush. Be careful in case the effervescence causes splashing.

BATHROOM DRAIN CLEANER

The following composition helps to dissolve scum and hair in sluggish bathroom sink and tub drains.

BATHROOM DRAIN FLUSH

1 cup baking soda
1 cup salt
½ cup white vinegar
2 quarts boiling water

Pour the baking soda, salt, and vinegar into the drain. Let work for about 15 minutes; be careful in case the bubbling action causes splashing. Flush the drain with the boiling water, followed by hot tap water for 1 minute. The baking soda, salt, and vinegar can also be used as a combination toilet bowl scrub and toilet drain cleaner.

SEPTIC TANK TREATMENT

To keep your septic system working smoothly and to help avoid clogging, backups, corrosion, and septic odors, flush one cup of baking soda down the toilet every week. You must do this on a regular basis since the dissolved sodium bicarbonate is forced out of the septic tank every time new material enters.

BAKING SODA IN THE NURSERY

BABY CLOTHES FRESHENER

Clean baby clothes that have been in storage can be freshened without having to be laundered by briefly soaking them in a solution of ½ cup baking soda per gallon of water, rinsing, and then gently drying.

BABY SHOES CLEANER

Clean white baby shoes with baking soda sprinkled on a damp sponge. Rinse with a clean damp sponge, dry, and buff lightly. Polish if necessary.

NURSERY SPOTTER

When baby leaves milk, food, or spit-up stains on clothes, bibs, or bedding, pretreat with a paste of three parts baking soda per one part water until the item can be washed. In addition to loosening the stains, this will prevent the formation of sour odors.

NURSERY PRESOAK

For items like dirty cloth diapers that require deep cleaning, presoak for an hour or two in a bath of ½ cup baking soda in 1 gallon of water.

CHANGING PAD CLEANER

Routinely clean plastic changing pads by wiping with a solution of one tablespoon baking soda per cup of water.

DIAPER PAIL FRESHENERS

Sprinkle each addition to the diaper pail liberally with baking soda to control odors until emptying.

When the plastic diaper pail picks up odors, clean and deodorize it by adding one cup baking soda and then filling with warm water. Let this solution sit for an hour or two, then rinse and air dry.

PRICKLY HEAT/DIAPER RASH SOOTHER

Sooth prickly heat by giving baby a sponge bath with a solution of one tablespoon baking soda per quart of water. After bathing, gently pat the baby dry with a soft towel.

This same solution can be used as a bath soak to soothe mild diaper rash.

VOMIT CLEANUP

If baby (or older child) vomits and you cannot clean it immediately, cover it with baking soda to control the smell (and sight) until you can get to it.

ACCIDENT CLEANUP

If baby (or older child) wets the bed at night, first blot the wet mattress with a towel. Then sprinkle the damp area with baking soda. Let it dry thoroughly and then vacuum.

STUFFED TOY CLEANER

Baby's favorite stuffed animals often seem to attract more than their share of dirt and smells, and most are not machine washable. When it's time for a cleaning, place the stuffed toy in a large plastic bag, add ½ cup of baking soda, close the bag, and shake vigorously. Remove from the bag and shake as much baking soda as possible from the animal; remove the rest with a hairbrush.

Clean vinyl-covered stuffed toys with a solution of one tablespoon baking soda per cup of water. Remove stains with a little baking soda on a damp sponge.

PLASTIC DOLL BATH

Freshen old doll clothes by soaking them in a solution of three tablespoons baking soda per quart of water, rinsing, and then air drying. Plastic dolls themselves can be cleaned of dirt and stains with a toothbrush and paste of three parts baking soda to one part gentle dishwashing liquid or liquid soap. Rinse well and dry.

PLASTIC TOY CLEANER

Clean plastic toys, especially those that see hard service outdoors, with baking soda sprinkled on a damp sponge or by soaking in a solution of four tablespoons baking soda and a few drops of gentle dishwashing liquid per quart of water. (Check first for paper decals, which could wash off.) Rinse well and dry. For spot cleaning of stains and errant crayon, pen, or marker "decorations," try scouring with a paste of three parts baking soda to one part gentle dishwashing liquid or liquid soap. Rinse well and dry.

BABY BOTTLE DEODORIZER

To remove lingering sour milk or juice odors from baby bottles, add two tablespoons of baking soda, fill with hot water, shake or stir to dissolve the baking soda, and let soak for at least a couple of hours (overnight if possible). Rinse well and wash as usual.

CRAYON REMOVER

Remove crayon marks from washable walls and floors by gentle scrubbing with baking soda on a damp sponge or nylon scrubber.

BAKING SODA IN THE LAUNDRY

FABRIC SOFTENER

Add ½ cup of baking soda with your detergent to the wash load to make the clothes feel soft and smell fresh.

FABRIC FRESHENER

Presoak smelly items that require extra attention, like cloth diapers, gardening clothes, or whatever you were wearing for that close encounter with the skunk, for an hour or two in a solution of ½ cup baking soda in 1 gallon of water. This will help remove stains and odors.

RING-AROUND-THE-COLLAR

As a prewash treatment for dirty cuffs, collars, and mildew stains on stored clothing, scrub with a paste of three parts baking soda to two parts white vinegar. Maintain adequate ventilation.

DELICATES

Hand washables and delicates that have acquired a stale odor in storage need not be laundered. Just soak in four tablespoons baking soda per quart of water, rinse well, squeeze, and air dry.

Hand washables and delicates that do need laundering can be washed in a solution of one teaspoon gentle dishwashing liquid and two tablespoons baking soda per quart of water. Rinse and dry as usual.

DRY CLEANABLES

Many "dry clean only" items, like scarves and pants, can be safely cleaned and freshened between visits to the cleaner's by washing in a solution of four tablespoons baking soda per quart of cold water, followed by thorough rinsing and gentle drying. Test for colorfastness and shrinkage first.

HAMPERS

Between washes, keep hampers odor free by sprinkling baking soda on each layer of added clothing. This is especially effective with grimy work or athletic wear, and will keep the hamper itself from picking up odors. The baking soda added to the washing machine with the dirty clothes will help them come out soft and fresh smelling.

LAUNDRY BLUING

Before the days of fluorescent whiteners in laundry detergents, bluing was often used to make whites whiter. This was based on centuries of experience in the arts where it was discovered that adding a very small amount of blue will make white appear whiter. You can do this with ultramarine blue, a chemical dye available in artist supply stores. If you prefer to launder with soap flakes instead of synthetic detergents and would like some extra "natural" whitening, try the following:

LAUNDRY BLUING

3½ cups baking soda
1 cup corn syrup
½ teaspoon ultramarine blue

Mix the ingredients well and store in a covered container. Use a scant ½ teaspoon per load of whites. Mix into the water before adding the clothes. This is a dye, so do not add directly to clothes.

BAKING SODA AROUND THE HOUSE

ROOM DEODORIZER

A tobacco smoke–filled room can be made more comfort-
able with a baking soda deodorizer spray. Fill a plant
mister bottle with a solution of four tablespoons baking
soda per quart of warm water. Mist the smoky air to
reduce the haze and the smell.

MULTIPURPOSE CLEANERS

These are cleaners for virtually any washable hard surface around the house, including windows, counters,
appliances, tile floors and walls, marble tabletops, vinyl
floors, etc. They can also be used for spot cleaning spills
and stains.

ALL-PURPOSE CLEANER I

¼ cup baking soda
1 cup clear ammonia
½ cup white vinegar
1 gallon warm water

Mix the ingredients together well. Use rubber gloves and
maintain adequate ventilation. Apply the solution to
soiled surfaces with a sponge, mop, or paper towel; rinse
and dry. For stuck-on soils, scour with a nylon scrubber.
For windows and mirrors, wipe on the solution with a
paper towel, let dry to a powdery haze, and wipe clean
with a dry paper towel.

ALL-PURPOSE CLEANER II

If you dislike the way vinegar and ammonia smell, try this instead.

¼ cup baking soda
¼ cup lemon juice
⅛ cup borax
1 tablespoon gentle dishwashing liquid
1 gallon warm water

Mix the ingredients together well and use as you would All-Purpose Cleaner I (page 42). You can pour some of this into a spray bottle and use it for spot cleaning hard surfaces.

WALL CLEANER

Clean washable walls with a solution of one cup baking soda and one tablespoon gentle dishwashing liquid in one gallon of hot water.

UPHOLSTERY AND CARPET CLEANERS

Before using any cleaning preparation on carpeting or upholstery, first check colorfastness in an inconspicuous area.

Absorb fresh greasy stains on carpets and cloth upholstery with equal parts baking soda and salt, or clean with a paste of three parts baking soda per one part water. Sprinkle the powder on the stain, brush lightly, leave for a few hours, then vacuum. Rub the paste into the stain, let dry, then brush or vacuum away.

For coffee or tea stains try a solution of two table-

spoons baking soda and one tablespoon borax per pint of water.

To clean and deodorize carpets and cloth upholstery, be sure the surface is dry, sprinkle on baking soda liberally, let sit for about fifteen minutes, and then vacuum thoroughly. For particularly musty smells, leave the baking soda on longer or use a blend of one part each baking soda, borax, and cornmeal.

For carpets that are musty or mildewed from having been wet, dry thoroughly and sprinkle baking soda liberally beneath (if not tacked) and on top. Let sit overnight, then vacuum. Repeat if necessary.

VINYL UPHOLSTERY CLEANER

A solution of four tablespoons baking soda per quart of water or baking soda sprinkled on a damp sponge will remove oils and grease that can embrittle vinyl. For tough stains, scrub with a paste of three parts baking soda, one part water, and a few drops of gentle dishwashing liquid or liquid soap. Rinse with clear water and wipe dry.

LEATHER MILDEW REMOVER

For mildewed leather (not suede) upholstery or clothing, rub on a paste of three parts baking soda to one part water, let dry overnight, then gently brush or vacuum away. The leather will have to be repolished after this cleaning.

BASEBOARD CLEANER

The white metal baseboards that have replaced old-fashioned radiators can get spotted and smudged with grease, errant spray polish, splashed floor wax, and dirt. Make baseboards white again with baking soda sprinkled on a damp sponge or nylon scrubber. Tough jobs can be handled with a paste of three parts baking soda, one part water, and a few drops of gentle dishwashing liquid. Rinse well and dry.

MARBLE TOP STAINS
Safely scour stained marble on furniture tops with baking soda sprinkled on a damp sponge. Let the paste sit a few minutes, then rinse with warm water and dry.

WAX REMOVER
Remove crayon and other waxy marks, as from candles or paraffin, from most hard washable surfaces with a paste of three parts baking soda per one part water and a nylon scrubber.

ASHTRAY TREATMENT
Clean and deodorize ashtrays with a solution of four tablespoons baking soda per quart of water. Then sprinkle some baking soda into the clean, dry ashtray to prevent smoldering and reduce the odor of ashes.

LITTER BOX DEODORANT
Baking soda sprinkled on the bottom of the litter box before adding litter will help control odors. Use about one cup baking soda per three pounds of litter.

If you can't attend to used litter as quickly as you would like, cover with baking soda and stir slightly. This will control odors for a couple of hours.

PET BEDDING DEODORIZER

To clean and deodorize cloth pet bedding between launderings, first make sure it is dry, then sprinkle liberally with baking soda and let sit for fifteen to thirty minutes. Shake out or vacuum up the baking soda. For stronger odors, leave the baking soda on longer.

PET CAGE CLEANER

Clean and deodorize cages for birds and other pets with baking soda sprinkled on a damp sponge or nylon scrubber. Rinse well and dry. Do this when the pet is elsewhere, as when you change papers or litter.

PUPPY TRAINING AID

If you use the newspaper approach to puppy housebreaking, sprinkle the wet newspapers liberally with baking soda before discarding. This will minimize the odor.

PET ACCIDENT DEODORIZER

If your pet has had an accident or vomited on carpeting or cloth upholstered furniture, there will be a lingering odor that the animal may be able to detect even if you cannot. To avoid a repeat performance, shampoo the spot as quickly and thoroughly as possible. When completely dry, check for colorfastness, then sprinkle liberally with baking soda. Let sit for fifteen minutes, then vacuum thoroughly.

DOG DRY CLEANER

To clean and deodorize your dog when you can't give

him a bath, rub baking soda thoroughly into his coat
(make sure he's dry), then brush it out.

METAL CLEANERS

Baking soda can be used to clean and polish most metal
fixtures and decorations in the home. Gently clean and
polish chrome, stainless steel, silver, and gold plating
with baking soda sprinkled on a damp sponge or a simple paste of three parts baking soda per one part water.
Do not use on decorative aluminum, or lacquered brass,
bronze, or copper.

ASH METAL POLISH

Try this if you have a ready supply of ashes from a fire-
place or woodstove. The ashes supply alkali and extra
abrasion for tough jobs.

4 tablespoons baking soda
2 cups wood ashes

Mix well and store in a closed container. To use, mix a
portion with just enough water to form a paste. Rub on
soiled metals with a damp sponge or soft cloth. Rinse
and dry.

Electrolytic Silver Cleaner

A quick way to clean tarnished sterling silver or silver-
plated pieces en masse without resorting to polishing
one piece at a time with chemicals or abrasives is to
remove the black silver sulfide tarnish "electrically." This
is only for solid pieces with a shiny finish.

Place a piece of aluminum foil in the bottom of a large nonaluminum pan or the kitchen sink. Add a solution of one tablespoon baking soda or one teaspoon baking soda plus one teaspoon salt per quart of boiling water. Immerse the silver, making sure there is enough hot solution to cover it completely. With the silver in contact with the aluminum, an electric cell is formed, causing the silver sulfide (the black tarnish) to dissolve. After a few minutes the silver pieces should be tarnish-free. If not, the process can be repeated with fresh solution. This process will remove the dark accents in design crevices, which you may or may not like. Rinse the freshly cleaned silver, then buff it dry with a soft cloth. This process will leave a somewhat duller luster than a regular polish. If you prefer a high shine and don't mind polishing each piece individually, use the electrolytic method to remove the tarnish from a number of pieces at once, then polish them to a high shine one at a time with a commercial polish.

Verdigris Remover

Unlacquered copper easily forms the green tarnish of toxic copper carbonate known as verdigris. This is why copper pans are often lined with other metals like stainless steel, chromium, and tin. On unlined copper cookware, verdigris will form from reaction with certain acidic foods. Verdigris can be removed from copper, brass, and bronze with a mixture of baking soda and enough lemon juice to make a paste. After scouring, rinse well and dry. This will clean and brighten the metal.

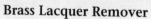

Brass Lacquer Remover

Most decorative brass produced in recent years is sold with a protective lacquer coating to keep it bright and shiny without polishing. In fact, cleaners and polishes should not be used on lacquered items; they should be cleaned with just a dust cloth and occasional damp sponge. If the lacquer cracks and peels it must be removed and the item relacquered (you can buy lacquering spray at the hardware store). To remove peeling lacquer, submerge the brass item in a bucket containing a solution of ½ cup baking soda per each gallon of boiling water. Leave the item in the solution until it cools to room temperature, then peel the lacquer off.

RUNNING SHOE DEODORANT

Minimize the odor of running shoes and other athletic footwear between uses by sprinkling two to four tablespoons of baking soda over the entire insole. Shake out the baking soda before wearing the shoes.

BOOK DEODORANT

If a treasured book has picked up a musty smell from damp basement storage or after having been wet, thoroughly dry it, then sprinkle a little baking soda between the pages and leave it there several days before brushing it out.

COMPUTER MOUSE CLEANER

Your computer mouse will work erratically if the ball it rolls on becomes dirty. Instead of using the harsher solvent-based cleaners normally recommended, remove the

ball from the mouse and clean it with baking soda sprinkled on a damp sponge. Rinse well and dry thoroughly.

POOR MAN'S PLASTER
To temporarily fill cracks in plaster, add just enough white craft glue to baking soda to make a paste. Work this into the crack with your finger and smooth the surface.

ROACH KILLER
Probably the safest preparation (to humans) for killing roaches and silverfish is a blend of equal parts baking soda and sugar. The sugar gets the bugs to eat the mixture and the large amount of baking soda they consume in relation to their weight kills them. Sprinkle the powder in infested areas. Although this blend is innocuous to warm-blooded species, it is best to keep children and pets away from it as you would any insect poison.

BAKING SODA IN THE YARD

SPORTS BALL CLEANER
Clean volleyballs, soccer balls, golf balls, bowling balls, bocci balls, and even baseballs with baking soda sprinkled on a damp sponge. Rinse and dry.

SPORTS EQUIPMENT CLEANER
Clean plastic, fiberglass, and painted aluminum sporting equipment with a paste of three parts baking soda per one

part water. This removes most spots and stains. Follow by washing with a mild detergent, then rinsing and drying.

SWING SET CLEANER
The plastic seats of your child's swing set are subject to environmental assaults ranging from tree sap and bird droppings to soot. Clean periodically with baking soda sprinkled on a damp sponge or a paste of three parts baking soda, one part water, and a few drops of gentle dishwashing liquid.

PATIO UMBRELLA AND FURNITURE CLEANER
The plastic mesh umbrella that shades your patio or deck table collects the same type of environmental grime as your child's swing set. After you check for colorfastness, clean it with a sponge and a solution of ½ cup baking soda and one tablespoon gentle dishwashing liquid in one gallon of hot water. Rinse well and let air dry. Use this solution to clean all of your plastic and glass patio or deck furniture.

ALUMINUM CLEANER
Aluminum screens, doors, and furniture, whether painted or unpainted, can be cleaned with a solution of ¼ cup baking soda per gallon of warm water. (The unpainted aluminum is already oxidized, so this solution will not harm it.) Cleaned painted aluminum benefits from a periodic coating of low or no abrasive automobile wax.

COOKOUT FLAME EXTINGUISHER
When you barbecue meat, fat dripping on hot coals can cause flames to shoot up to the food. To control this, put

a solution of one teaspoon baking soda in one pint of water into a plastic spray bottle. Spray it at the base of the flames as needed; it is more effective than water alone. This can also be brought on camping trips to ensure that the campfire is completely extinguished.

POOL WATER STABILIZER

The pH and alkalinity of swimming pool water should be controlled to maintain water clarity, provide optimum disinfection by the chlorine, and avoid eye sting. Baking soda is an effective alternative to the chemicals sold in pool supply stores to adjust alkalinity and pH. At the beginning of the season, if the pool water is below the minimum acceptable pH of 7.2, add 3 to 4 pounds of baking soda for every 10,000 gallons of water. Check the pH every week. If the pH is at least 7.2 but below 7.5—a condition where eye irritation and burning can be a problem—add 2 pounds of baking soda for each 10,000 gallons of water to raise the pH. To prevent clouding, especially in hard water areas or when using a calcium chlorinating agent, keep the pH below 7.8. In order to control pH without fluctuation, adequate alkalinity should be maintained. Alkalinity should be kept in the 110 to 150 ppm range for stabilized chlorinated isocyanates and 60 to 110 ppm for other chlorinating agents. Each 1½ pounds of baking soda adds 10 ppm alkalinity for every 10,000 gallons of water.

GARDEN FUNGICIDE

As a nontoxic alternative to chemical fungicides, spray a

solution of four teaspoons baking soda per gallon of water on rosebushes to prevent damage by black spot fungus. If you like, add a few drops of liquid soap to the solution to help spread it more evenly on the leaves.

This same spray can be used on grapes and vines to help prevent grape fungi, especially black rot, from forming. Apply once when the fruit starts to appear and then once a week for about two months. Reapply after each rain.

POTTING SOIL ALKALIZER

To flourish, some potted plants (like carnations, mums, and petunias) prefer a neutral soil. Home gardeners can raise the alkalinity of acid potting soil safely with a solution of four tablespoons baking soda per quart of water. This should be used sparingly, not as a routine treatment. A high accumulation of sodium salts in the soil is harmful to some plants.

GARDEN GREENER

If outdoor garden plants and bushes are fading, make them green again with the following:

1 teaspoon baking soda
1 teaspoon Epsom salts
½ teaspoon clear ammonia
1 gallon water

Mix the ingredients together well and store in an airtight container. Apply when needed at the rate of about 1 quart per rosebush-size shrub.

BAKING SODA IN THE PLAYROOM

PLAY CLAY

When you're through cleaning with baking soda, play with it.

2 cups baking soda
1 cup cornstarch
1¼ cups cold water
Food coloring, as desired

Blend the baking soda and cornstarch in a saucepan. Add the water and food coloring, if desired, and cook over medium heat, stirring constantly. When the mixture is the consistency of mashed potatoes, turn out on a plate and cover with a damp cloth. When cool enough to handle, it is ready to use. To preserve objects made from this clay, air dry them for 24 hours. (Thick pieces may take longer.) The drying of thin pieces can be accelerated by placing them in a preheated 350-degree oven for 15 minutes. Rapid drying of thin objects or oven drying of thicker objects will cause cracks. Dried pieces can be painted with watercolors, poster paints, or felt tip pens, and then coated with shellac, varnish, liquid plastic, or nail polish. Store unused clay in a tightly sealed plastic bag in the refrigerator, but warm to room temperature before use.

STALAGMITES AND STALACTITES

In underground caves, minerals dissolved in slowly dripping water form stalactites (growing down from the ceiling) and stalagmites (seeming to grow up from the ground). This process is easily demonstrated using baking soda and a few simple props:

Household glue
2 small glass baby food–size jars
1 large, flat disposable plastic plate
Hot water
6 teaspoons baking soda
1 14-inch piece of wool yarn

Glue the 2 jars to the plate about 4 inches apart. Fill the jars with hot water and dissolve 3 teaspoons of baking soda in each. Put the ends of the yarn in the solution in each jar, allowing the middle to hang between the jars while remaining at least ½ inch above the plate. Let sit undisturbed for 2 or 3 days—by that time stalactites will have formed on the yarn and stalagmites beneath it. This happens because the baking soda solution travels up the yarn and drips onto the plate. The drops on the plate evaporate, leaving behind a stalagmite of baking soda. Water evaporating from the solution dripping from the yarn creates stalactites.

COLOR MAGIC
Impress your friends with this baking soda trick. All you need is:

1 tablespoon liquid from a jar of pickled shredded red cabbage (see Note)
½ cup water
1 large water glass
1 teaspoon baking soda

Drain the dark purple liquid from the cabbage into a clean bowl. Pour the water into the glass. Add 1 tablespoon of the cabbage juice and stir. The water should be purple. Add the baking soda and swirl the liquid gently. At first it will fizz, and when the bubbles clear, the water will be a deep blue! The science behind this magic is hidden in the red cabbage. This vegetable contains a chemical that is sensitive to acids and alkalies. In acid solutions (like the vinegar and water from the jar) the chemical is purple. In alkaline solutions (like the one you made by adding the baking soda) it turns blue.

Note: The ingredients on the cabbage jar should include water and vinegar. There might be others—like salt, sugar, corn syrup, and citric acid—but these won't interfere with the magic.

MUMMIES

The ancient Egyptians preserved the bodies of their pharaohs with a mineral called natron, which is a natural blend of sodium bicarbonate, sodium carbonate, and sodium chloride, with small amounts of other salts. Natron was highly prized because it would remove all of the liquid—water, oils, and fat—from the body tissues, which was essential to prevent decay. The cleaned body was buried in a pile of natron for forty days before it was wrapped and entombed. Some of these mummies are still around today.

You can make your own mummies using the following recipe. Washing soda is sodium carbonate. You can find it in the laundry products aisle in the supermarket.

½ cup baking soda
½ cup washing soda
¼ cup table salt
1 apple

Mix the baking soda, washing soda, and salt in a small bowl. Cut the apple into 4 equal pieces. Carefully bury one of the apple quarters in the baking soda mixture. Make sure it is completely covered. Every 2 days, check that the apple is drying out and then rebury it. After 10 days, you'll have a mummified (a very dry) piece of apple. The apple, like a mummy, will last for a long time (though it wouldn't taste very good to eat).

SUBMARINE SEEDS

Eat the pieces of apple that you didn't mummify above, but save the seeds for the following:

½ cup water
1 large water glass
⅔ teaspoon baking soda
Apple seeds
1 tablespoon lemon juice or white vinegar

Pour the water into the glass. Add the baking soda and stir until dissolved. Add the apple seeds. Add the lemon juice or vinegar and stir gently. The seeds will rise and fall in the water as they are carried to the surface by carbon dioxide bubbles and then dropped as the bubbles burst.

BALLOON BLOWER

Tired of blowing up party balloons? Let baking soda do it for you.

1 balloon
2 tablespoons water
1 teaspoon baking soda
1 clean empty soda bottle
4 tablespoons lemon juice or white vinegar

Stretch the balloon a few times to make it easier to inflate. Add the water and baking soda to the bottle. Add the lemon juice or vinegar, then quickly fit the balloon over the mouth of the bottle. The carbon dioxide released from the baking soda inflates the balloon.

BAKING SODA IN THE GARAGE

Baking soda can be used in a number of ways to keep your car, motorcycle, boat, and the garage in which they're housed looking good.

WINDSHIELD AND CHROME CLEANER

To remove dead bugs, sap, bird droppings, tar, and traffic grime from chrome, windshields, and headlights, scrub with baking soda on a damp sponge and wipe with a paper towel. If a little more power is needed, try a paste of three parts baking soda and a few drops of gentle dishwashing liquid to one part water. Rinse well and dry. For big jobs try the following:

ALL-PURPOSE CLEANER

½ cup baking soda
1 cup clear ammonia
½ cup white vinegar
1 gallon warm water

Mix the ingredients together well. Use rubber gloves and maintain adequate ventilation. Wipe on the cleaner with a paper towel, let dry to a powdery haze, and wipe off with a clean paper towel. Use a nylon scrubber for careful spot scrubbing if necessary.

VINYL AND CANVAS CLEANERS

Remove oils and grease that can embrittle vinyl seating with a solution of four tablespoons baking soda per quart of water or baking soda sprinkled on a damp sponge. Rinse with water and wipe dry.

To remove tree sap, bird droppings, and general traffic grime from vinyl tops and canvas convertible car and boat tops, scrub with a paste of three parts baking soda per part of water and a soft bristle scrub brush. For more resistant soils, add a few drops of gentle dishwashing liquid to the baking soda paste. Follow with a mild detergent wash, rinse well, and dry.

AUTO/BOAT DEODORIZER

If your car or boat suffers from lingering odors from smoke, mildew, or children and pets, sprinkle baking soda liberally on all dry carpeting and cloth upholstery surfaces. Leave on overnight if possible and then vacuum. Then wash all nonabsorbent surfaces with a solution of four tablespoons baking soda per quart of water, rinse, and dry.

Cover the bottom of ashtrays with baking soda to control smoke odors and to quickly extinguish smoldering butts.

AUTO FLOOR CLEANERS
Absorb greasy stains on auto carpeting (and cloth upholstery) with equal parts baking soda and salt or clean them with a paste of three parts baking soda per one part water. Sprinkle the powder on the stain, brush lightly, leave for a few hours, then vacuum. Rub the paste into the stain, let dry, then brush or vacuum away.

For musty or mildewed carpet, dry thoroughly first, then sprinkle baking soda liberally beneath (if it can be lifted) and on top and let sit overnight before vacuuming. Repeat if necessary.

NAUTICAL BRASS CLEANERS
Unlacquered brass fittings on boats can be cleaned and brightened by applying a mixture of baking soda and enough lemon juice to make a paste. Rub on and leave for a few minutes. Then rinse well with warm water and dry.

Fittings of unlacquered brass (an alloy containing copper) can form the green tarnish of copper carbonate known as verdigris. Remove verdigris from brass with the baking soda and lemon juice paste above. After scouring, rinse well and dry.

FIBERGLASS BODY CLEANER

Clean stains and grime on fiberglass car and boat body panels by scrubbing with baking soda on a damp sponge, followed by rinsing and drying. For extra tough stains, leave on the wet baking soda after scrubbing until it dries, then wipe away the powder.

GARAGE FLOOR SPOTTER

Use baking soda alone or in combination with mason's sand, cornmeal, or diatomaceous earth (from your pool supply dealer), to absorb spilled oil and grease from the garage floor. Any traces of stain can be cleaned by wetting the area and scouring with baking soda and a scrub brush.

BATTERY TERMINAL CLEANER

Clean corroded battery posts and cable connectors with a paste of three parts baking soda per one part water. After cleaning and drying, lightly coat with petroleum jelly.

AUTO AND BOAT FIRE EXTINGUISHER

Keep a large box of baking soda handy in the car, boat, and garage for extinguishing small oil, gas, and engine fires. From a safe distance, throw the baking soda at the base of the flames. If the fire is too large or intense to respond quickly to the baking soda, call the fire department immediately.

BAKING SODA IN THE MEDICINE CHEST

SHAMPOO
When your hair is suffering from dandruff or conditioner overload, you can rejuvenate it without the commercial concoctions. Instead of shampooing, wet your hair and vigorously rub in a handful of baking soda. Be sure to massage it into your scalp as well. Rinse thoroughly and air dry if possible or blow-dry at the coolest setting. Your hair might look dry at first, but regular washing (which should be no less frequent than every other day if you have a dandruff problem) with baking soda should eliminate dandruff and soften your hair. Once your hair and scalp have returned to a naturally healthy state, alternate washing with baking soda and baby shampoo.

ANTICHLORINE HAIR RINSE
Overchlorinated pool water can leave hair dull or discolored. After swimming, counteract chlorine's effects by rinsing your hair with a solution of ½ teaspoon baking soda per pint of water.

EYE RELIEF
For relief from smoke or pollution-irritated eyes, use an eyewash cup or sterile eyedropper to apply a solution of a scant ⅛ teaspoon of baking soda per cup of sterile water. Do not store; make fresh solution as needed.

CONTACT LENS STORAGE FLUID
If you run out of your storage fluid, try this solution for

keeping your hard contact lenses lubricated between wearings.

HARD CONTACT LENS FLUID

¼ teaspoon baking soda
¼ teaspoon salt
1 cup sterile water

Mix well in a sterile container until the baking soda and salt are dissolved. Pour the solution through a paper coffee filter to remove any undissolved particles and store in a sterile dropper bottle.

GROOMING AIDS CLEANER

Clean cosmetic sponges, combs, hairbrushes, plastic curlers, and makeup applicators gently by soaking overnight in a solution of baking soda alone (four tablespoons baking soda per quart of water) or with a few drops of liquid soap. Soak sponges or makeup applicators separate from other items. For natural bristle brushes, a tablespoon of clear ammonia can be added to the baking soda and liquid soap; use a covered container or be certain there is adequate ventilation for soaking. Plastic combs can be cleaned and disinfected by using the baking soda soaking solution above with three tablespoons of household bleach added. Be careful not to get this on bleach sensitive surfaces. **Never mix bleach with liquid soap or ammonia.**

EARWAX SOFTENER

If you are bothered by excessive buildup of hardened earwax, apply a few drops of this softener at bedtime.

EARWAX SOFTENER

¼ teaspoon baking soda
½ cup glycerine (from the pharmacy)
1 cup sterile water

Mix well in a sterile container until clear. Store in a sterile dropper bottle.

MOUTHWASH/GARGLE

Rinsing or gargling with a solution of one teaspoon baking soda in ½ cup of water is as effective as most commercial preparations.

TEETH/GUM CLEANERS

As the ever-increasing popularity of commercial baking soda toothpastes indicates, baking soda is a safe and effective way to keep your teeth and gums clean and healthy. A little baking soda on a wet toothbrush provides all the cleaning and polishing action you need. It deodorizes and neutralizes acidic bacterial wastes.

Some people do not care for the taste of baking soda alone and add a drop or two of flavoring oils or extracts, like peppermint and anise. Some prefer baking soda with enough mashed strawberry to form a paste. Strawberries are supposed to have dental stain-removing properties of their own.

For extra whitening and antibacterial action, brush with a paste of three parts baking soda and one part hydrogen peroxide, paying extra attention to cleaning at the gum line.

DENTURE CLEANER
Soak dentures in a solution of four tablespoons baking soda per quart of water or scrub them with baking soda on a wet toothbrush.

CANKER SORE RELIEF
Canker sores are a result of viral infection, but it is an overlying bacterial infection that causes the painful whitish sore. Neutralize the bacteria by gently rinsing your mouth with a solution of one teaspoon baking soda in ½ glass of warm water. This will also help relieve the pain.

PRESHAVE/AFTERSHAVE
For those with sensitive skin, a solution of one table-spoon baking soda per cup of water makes a soothing preshave or aftershave splash that can minimize irritating razor burns.

BLACKHEAD TREATMENT
To loosen blackheads, mix equal parts baking soda and water and apply. Rub gently for two or three minutes, then rinse with very warm water. Do not squeeze.

LEG SHAVING AID
A solution of one tablespoon baking soda per cup of

water is an alternative to shaving cream or soap and water for shaving your legs with a safety razor.

FOOT BATH

A ten-minute soak in a solution of four tablespoons baking soda per quart of warm water will relieve tired feet, soften calluses, and soothe the itch of athlete's foot.

ATHLETE'S FOOT CARE

Athlete's foot is caused by fungi and yeast that can proliferate in the hot, sweaty environment in shoes. The best prevention is to keep feet dry by wearing absorbent socks and correctly fitting shoes that are made of a breathable material like leather, lightly dusting feet with baking soda to reduce moisture from perspiration, and in hot and humid weather soak in the Foot Bath (above). If you have athlete's foot, add just enough tepid water to baking soda to form a paste and rub it into the affected area, especially between the toes. Rinse, dry thoroughly, and apply an over-the-counter athlete's foot treatment.

FOOT SMOOTHER

Smooth and soften hard and rough areas on the feet, such as heels and calluses, by massaging them with a paste of three parts baking soda per one part water. Follow with a baking soda Foot Bath (see above), rinse, and dry thoroughly.

NAIL CARE

Toe- and fingernails can be kept clean by scrubbing with

a wet nailbrush dipped into baking soda. This will soften cuticles too.

BATH SALTS
There is little to rival the relaxing effect of soaking in a hot bath, especially after working, exercising, or playing hard. While you're soaking, dissolve ½ cup of baking soda in the bath water to clean away dirt and perspiration and neutralize body odors. Those who wish to be extra pampered—or who are extra sore—can try the following:

BUBBLING BATH SALTS

2½ cups baking soda
2 cups cream of tartar
½ cup cornstarch
A few drops of perfume (optional)

Mix well and store in a covered container. Use ¼ cup per bathful.

RHEUMATIC BATH SALTS
This will help sore and tired muscles feel better.

2 cups baking soda
1 cup Epsom salts (magnesium sulfate)
½ cup salt

Mix well and store in a covered container. Use ½ cup per bathful.

SPONGE BATH

When there's no time for a shower or bath, freshen up with a quick sponge bath using a solution of four tablespoons baking soda per quart of water. This will neutralize odors and wash away dirt and perspiration.

KNEE AND ELBOW SCRUB

Scrub grimy dirt from children's elbows and knees with baking soda sprinkled on a damp washcloth.

DEODORANT

A natural alternative to deodorant sprays and lotions is simply to dust some baking soda under your arms to absorb perspiration and neutralize odors. This will save your clothes from deodorant stains as well.

BURNS AND RASHES

Generalized minor burns and rashes, like sunburn and prickly heat, can be relieved by soaking in a tepid bath containing one cup of baking soda. After soaking, do not rinse, just gently towel dry. If you haven't the time to soak, take a sponge bath using a solution of four tablespoons baking soda per quart of water.

Localized minor burns and rashes can be soothed with a wet compress of baking soda solution or a paste of three parts baking soda to one part water or witch hazel. Baking soda paste will also help relieve the itch of poison ivy.

Sunburn blisters can be treated with a sterile dressing soaked in the baking soda solution.

INSECT BITES AND STINGS

The pain and irritation of most common insect bites and stings can be relieved by quick application of baking soda mixed with just enough water, witch hazel, or clear ammonia to form a paste. Keep the paste moist by covering with a damp cloth or dressing.

ANTACIDS

The generations-old relief for acid indigestion and heartburn is baking soda. Baking soda contains sodium. If you suffer from hypertension or are on a salt-restricted diet, consult your health care professional before taking it internally. While baking soda is a natural choice for neutralizing stomach acids, it is not a remedy for other types of stomach problems such as nausea, stomachache, gas pains, abdominal cramps, or stomach distention (bloating) caused by overeating or overdrinking. Dissolve a level ½ teaspoon of baking soda in four fluid ounces of water and drink.

For those spoiled by the convenience and pleasant taste of prepared antacid liquids, try the following:

ANTACID LIQUID

1 tablespoon baking soda
1 teaspoon sugar
4 drops peppermint oil, or to taste
1 cup water

Mix well and store in an airtight bottle in the refrigerator for up to 1 month. When needed, take 1 or 2 tablespoons.

THE ALTERNATIVE BAKING SODA
ALTERNATIVE

Even baking soda aficionados are subject to the lure of convenience when using their favorite alternative to formulated cleaners. So now there is a new baking soda alternative. It comes in a handy container, it requires no mixing, and it even smells good. It's baking soda toothpaste, of course. Baking soda toothpaste is composed of three major ingredients: baking soda, water, and a mild detergent. A number of the preceding uses suggested a paste of baking soda, water, and a few drops of gentle dishwashing detergent or liquid soap. A baking soda toothpaste combines all three, in addition to some miscellaneous ingredients. When you can't keep a box of baking soda handy, try a tube of baking soda toothpaste instead. For the full baking soda benefit, use a paste rather than a gel product. The pastes generally contain a higher baking soda content.

The guidelines for using a baking soda toothpaste are the same as described earlier for using baking soda itself. Please review these commonsense recommendations once more. Remember to test-clean a small inconspicuous area first to check for colorfastness and general compatibility. **Handle baking soda toothpaste with the same care accorded any other household product. Above all, keep it out of the reach of children. It is designed to taste good but not to be ingested. This is particularly true of products containing fluoride. Sodium fluoride, the most widely used anticavity** ingredient, is harmless for brushing teeth but poisonous if ingested in a large enough quantity. Be sure to thoroughly rinse any food or food contact surface that is cleaned with a fluoride-containing toothpaste. A nonfluoride product is recommended for the uses described here.

ALL THROUGH THE HOUSE

The following can be cleaned of dirt, grime, mildew, and stains with a dab of baking soda toothpaste on a wet sponge or nylon scrubber. If the paste seems too dry or thick as you're rubbing it in, just sprinkle with a little water. In all cases, rinse well after scrubbing and then dry.

Hard-skinned fruit and vegetables (rinse well)
Stained plastic, glass, ceramic, or nonaluminum metal
    containers
Glass and stainless steel coffeepots
All nonaluminum and nonstick cookware
Plastic cups and dishes
Chinaware
Pewterware
Wood and plastic cutting boards (rinse well)
Ceramic tile countertops and backsplashes
Butcher-block counters and tabletops
Plastic laminate counters and tabletops
Plastic laminate table seams
Metal chair and table legs
Standard (not self- or continuous clean) ovens
Stovetops
Stove backsplashes

Electric range catch pans

"Fingerprinted" enamel appliances

Small plastic appliances (mixers, blenders, etc.)

Inside surfaces of refrigerators, freezers, automatic dishwashers, and microwave ovens

Door gaskets on refrigerators, freezers, and automatic dishwashers

Washable (plastic laminate, enamel) cabinets

Refrigerator drip tray

Vinyl upholstery

Black heel marks and crayon on linoleum and vinyl flooring

Stainless steel, porcelain, and enamel sinks

Baby's high chair

Glazed ceramic floor and wall tile

Tile grout

Fiberglass sinks, tubs and showers

Plastic shower curtains

Glass shower doors

Mirrors and windows

Metal, porcelain, and ceramic plumbing fixtures

Crayon and wax on washable hard surfaces

Metal baseboards

White baby shoes

Plastic dolls

Plastic toys (be careful around decals)

Pet cages (remove the pet first)

Marble top furniture

Unlacquered metals: chrome, stainless steel, silver, gold, pewter, copper, brass, bronze

Plastic, fiberglass, hard rubber, and painted aluminum
sports equipment
Golf balls, volleyballs, soccer balls, bocci balls, bowl-
ing balls, baseballs
Computer mouse ball (remove from mouse first)
Automobile windows, headlights, chrome, vinyl tops,
and canvas tops
Sap-stained auto paint (use sparingly and keep wet)
Fiberglass auto and boat panels
Plastic seats on swing sets
Plastic and glass patio furniture

THE
ENVIRONMENTAL
ALTERNATIVE

In recent years, the unique versatility of baking soda has been applied to no less an undertaking than the cleaning, deodorizing, and deacidifying of the environment. Baking soda combats acid rain as effectively as it curbs acid stomach. It is as safe in removing paint from an airliner as it is in polishing stains from your teeth. It is as effective in reducing lead in drinking water as it is in cleaning corrosion from a car battery. At a time when high-tech environmental solutions can be dangerous, baking soda is safe, effective, and economical.

MUNICIPAL WATER TREATMENT

Millions of Americans are exposed to lead-contaminated water every day. Detecting contamination is complicated because lead levels in drinking water can vary markedly between distribution systems in the same area, between houses supplied by the same system, between different types of taps, and at different times of day at a single tap.

Lead and other toxic metals enter drinking water that is corrosive to piping in the distribution system and the home. Corrosion occurs when the water is acidic (as from acid rain) or contains an oxidizing agent, such as chlorinating compounds or even just dissolved oxygen. Fortunately, lead can be controlled with sodium bicarbonate. Dissolved lead and bicarbonate react to form a durable, impermeable coating inside pipes that protects against further leaching of lead and other metals. With concern over the problem of lead poisoning in children increasing, sodium bicarbonate is becoming a major weapon in the fight to keep the nation's water safe and potable.

ACID LAKE RECOVERY

A side effect of acid rain is the formation of acid lakes. Most fish, and the aquatic organisms they eat, thrive only in neutral water. Too much acidity, or too much alkalinity, is fatal. Baking soda, the age-old treatment for relieving stomach acid, is proving to be the most effective treatment for acid lakes as well.

James Bisogni, Jr., a professor at Cornell University, was the first to recognize and demonstrate the obvious advantages of sodium bicarbonate. In 1985 he adopted as his laboratory Wolf Pond, a fifty-acre acid lake in the Adirondacks that could no longer support game fish. Only a small number of trash fish survived. The simple addition of approximately twenty tons of baking soda succeeded in neutralizing the acid and restoring the health of the lake.

ACID RAIN RELIEF

Both coal- and oil-burning power plants produce acid gas emissions when the sulfur contained in the fuel is released up the flue stack in the form of sulfur dioxide. This acid gas is ultimately returned to earth as acid rain. When finely ground sodium bicarbonate is injected into the acidic flue gases of power plant boilers, it can remove over 90 percent of the sulfur dioxide. The sodium bicarbonate reacts with the gas to form solid salt cake (sodium sulfate) plus steam and carbon dioxide.

WASTE TREATMENT

Sodium bicarbonate is used in municipal and industrial wastewater and sewage treatment plants to ensure proper biological control in waste digesters. Bacteria is used to reduce organic sludge and transform it into stable and compact solid residues. The drier and more compact these residues can be made, the less solid waste there is for disposal. Waste-digesting bacteria need a slightly alkaline environment to work efficiently, but their decomposition of certain wastes creates acids. If too much acid builds up, conversion of waste to solid residue slows down, producing a wet and bulky sludge for disposal. Sodium bicarbonate keeps digesters running efficiently by reducing acids, aids in toxic metals removal, and provides the odor control important to treatment plant neighbors.

PAINT STRIPPING

Sodium bicarbonate is used in a clever alternative to industrial-scale paint strippers. It eliminates the need for hazardous chemical or mineral processes and minimizes the creation, and disposal costs, of toxic waste.

There have traditionally been two basic alternatives

for stripping paint from large surfaces such as industrial equipment, metal superstructures, and aircraft: the use of chemical strippers containing toxic metals and sand blasting. Chemical strippers form a chemical sludge that requires costly disposal as hazardous waste, and they pose a contact and inhalation danger to workers. Sand blasting is fast, effective, and economical, but can generate hazardous silica dust. Blasting with minute plastic beads instead of sand removes the threat of silicosis, but retains dust inhalation problems.

During the restoration of the Statue of Liberty, a compressor was used to direct a stream of dry bicarb to clean the tar coating from the inside of the statue's delicate copper skin. Blasting with baking soda cleaned the copper without abrasion and without exposing workers in the statue to hazardous blasting media or chemicals. This led to the development of a new paint-stripping technique that takes full advantage of sodium bicarbonate's effective and safe cleaning properties: blasting with a pressurized slurry of baking soda in water. The slurry form minimizes dust generation and can be used on virtually all hard surfaces, including plastic composites. Because the bicarbonate is water soluble, it is easily washed from the coating waste, which can then be concentrated for disposal. The separated bicarbonate solution can be sewered, if local regulations allow, or recovered for additional use as an acid neutralizer in treating electroplating wastes or supplying alkalinity to sewage treatment plants.

On industrial plant sites, bicarb blasting is preferred because it can be used to remove rust, corrosion, and grease, in addition to coatings, and can be used safely on sensitive rotating and hard-to-reach equipment parts. This method of paint removal has also found growing acceptance in the aviation industry, where stripping paint from aircraft is vitally important to detect metal fatigue, cracks, corrosion, and other structural problems. As an alternative to the normal methylene chloride–based strippers, bicarbonate blasting has so far successfully addressed all safety, efficacy, environmental, and worker hygiene concerns at the same time as it has minimized waste disposal problems.

SOIL SAVER

Baking soda's safety, efficacy, and economy are not restricted to improving our air and water. It can be applied to contaminated soils with equal benefit. There are numerous sites in the United States and abroad where the ground itself bears detectable levels of hazardous chemicals. Of great concern are the various halogenated (i.e., containing chlorine or bromine) organic chemicals that have seeped into the ground at manufacturing sites and landfills, as well as pesticides that have accumulated after application or that have been inadvertently liberated during manufacture or disposal.

The standard treatment for contaminated ground is either removal to a special hazardous waste landfill or incineration. Transport to a designated landfill is not favored because it simply moves the hazard instead of eliminating it. Incineration is preferred because it destroys the chemical contaminants. While incineration would appear to be a straightforward approach, it is a logistical challenge that can become an economic nightmare. Once the extent of contamination has been determined, the entire volume of soil must be excavated and fed to the incinerator. Depending upon the amount of soil to be treated and its accessibility, incineration may be done on-site. Otherwise, it must be shipped by secure transport to an appropriate facility. Incineration costs can be as much as $2000 per ton on-site and up to 50 percent greater off-site.

The U.S. Environmental Protection Agency, in conjunction with the Navy's Civil Engineering Lab, has developed a baking soda solution to this environmental problem. They have invented an efficient, relatively inexpensive method for decomposing halogenated contaminants. This process involves crushing and screening the contaminated soil and then blending in sodium bicarbonate at 10 percent of its weight. This blend is then heated for about one hour at 630°F. The treated soil is nonhazardous and can be returned to the site of its excavation. Cleanup is done on-site, eliminating transportation costs and minimizing air emissions and toxic residual wastes. It is the safest and most effective chemical method available, and can be implemented for about 10 percent of the cost of incineration. Full-scale tests of this process are currently under way. They are expected to prove yet another success for baking soda in environmental management.

BAKING AND
BAKING SODA

A book on baking soda would not be complete without baking recipes and an explanation of how baking soda reacts with other common baking ingredients to such delicious ends. Most home-baked goods are composed of relatively few ingredients, namely flour, leavening, salt, liquids (usually water or milk), eggs, shortening, and sweeteners. A basic understanding of how these ingredients interact in a batter or dough helps explain why baking soda, alone or mixed with a baking acid to form baking powder, is used in preference to yeast or mechanical leavening (i.e., simply whipping in air) in some baked goods. For baking soda applications, I use the term "baked" broadly to encompass panfried foods like pancakes to deep-fried foods like doughnuts and fritters. The common denominator among all these foods is that flour is the major ingredient and the finished product has a crumb, or porous, texture.

FLOUR

Most home baking today is done with wheat flour because wheat is the only edible grain that provides sufficient gluten to trap leavening gases and allow for a raised product. Gluten is the plastic and elastic product of the grain's protein. Gluten is considered plastic because it will change its shape (stretch) under pressure and elastic because it will expand to incorporate the leavening carbon dioxide, air, or steam but will resist rupture. Good gluten development is of obvious value in bread dough but of lesser importance in cake and pastry doughs and batters. In general, the higher the wheat protein content, the higher its gluten content when mixed into a dough. Also, the higher the protein content, the harder the wheat kernel.

Three basic types of wheat are grown in the United States today. They are differentiated by their hardness and uses in food. The bulk of the American wheat crop, approximately 75 percent, is hard wheat intended for bread baking. Hard wheat flour is low in starch, high in protein, and forms a strong gluten. Soft wheat, accounting for about 20 percent of the harvest, has a lower protein content, more starch, and develops a weak gluten. Soft wheat flours are preferred for cakes and soda/acid leavened products in general. The balance of the U.S. crop is the especially hard durum wheat. Durum gluten is very strong but not sufficiently elastic for general use in bread. Durum is usually coarsely milled into the semolina used to make the stiff doughs needed for dried pastas.

Consumers, and even commercial bakers, do not usually buy flours that are actually labeled "hard wheat" or "soft wheat." The various wheat flours available in the supermarket or specialty foods store are designated as all-purpose, self-rising, whole wheat, bread, graham, unbleached, or bromated. These descriptions are based on the grinding and blending operations at the miller's.

The first step in converting grain to flour is milling. The wheat kernels are passed between two grooved rollers turning at different speeds. This shearing action separates the endosperm (starch and protein) from the bran and germ, which go on to separate grinding and sieving. The endosperm is crushed and ground to a mixture of coarse and fine flours. The fine flour is sieved off and the rest is further ground. This combination of grinding and sieving is repeated several times to collect all the fine flour possible. Semolina is made by collecting some of the coarse flour after the first milling. This semolina is a high protein flour for making dried pastas, but it has a weaker gluten than durum semolina.

Most baking flours are treated with a bleaching and aging agent. Bleaching ensures a uniform whiteness but also destroys the small amount of vitamin E in the flour. It also ages the flour by modifying its proteins to improve gluten formation. Some flours are not bleached but are still aged, with potassium bromate or potassium iodate, to improve their gluten. The last step before the final packaging of most white flour is addition of vitamin and mineral enrichment with niacin, thiamin, riboflavin, iron, and in some cases calcium.

COMMON WHEAT FLOURS

All-Purpose Flour. A bleached, enriched blend of hard and soft wheat flours intended for use in a wide range of foods.

Unbleached Flour. Unbleached (but aged) all-purpose flour.

Bread Flour. Hard wheat flour; some flours sold as bread flour have added barley malt flour (food for the yeast) and potassium bromate (for gluten development).

Bromated Flour. Hard wheat flour to which potassium

bromate has been added as a gluten developer. Bromated flours were developed primarily for biscuits but are also used for bread. They promote a faster rising and an airier loaf.

Hard Wheat Flour. Simply what its name indicates, hard wheat flour is produced in both white and whole wheat varieties. It is more likely found in a specialty food store than a supermarket and is used primarily for bread baking.

Whole Wheat Flour. A medium-fine hard wheat flour with the germ retained but the bran either partially or totally removed; used mostly for bread but can be mixed with white flour for nearly all nonpastry baking.

Graham Flour. The entire coarsely ground wheat kernel (endosperm, germ, and bran). This name is sometimes used loosely to include coarse whole wheat flours. It is used the same way as whole wheat flour.

Self-Rising Flour. Soft wheat flour blended with sodium bicarbonate, monocalcium phosphate, and salt. It is popular for making biscuits, muffins, and quick breads. Self-rising flour is sometimes sold as phosphated flour.

Cake Flour. Especially fine soft wheat flour that has been treated to weaken its gluten. This treatment allows incorporation of large amounts of shortening into batters and doughs, which encourages good crumb in cakes and flakiness in pastries. Soft wheat flours are also used commercially for making doughnuts, cookies, crackers, and pretzels.

Gluten Flour. White flour from which nearly all the starch has been removed. It is expensive and intended for dietetic purposes, but it can be used in small amounts in breads made from grains like rye and barley that have little or no gluten.

OTHER FLOURS

While much less commonly available than wheat flours, meals and flours from other nutritional sources are becoming increasingly popular.

Rye Flour. Varies from a light flour, milled from endosperm, to a very dark flour, milled from the whole grain and suitable for pumpernickel. Rye flour sold for bread baking may contain some hard wheat flour.

Barley Flour. A light, high protein, very low gluten flour milled from whole hulled barley.

Triticale Flour. A low gluten wheat-rye crossbreed produced for developing countries because of its high protein content. Although perishable and not widely available in this country, it is a good pastry flour and useful for high protein bread. Gentler kneading is required.

Soy Flour. In the strictest sense, this is flour milled from raw soybeans while soya flour is milled from toasted soybeans. Soy flour is generally milled from whole soybeans into one of three types of flour: full-fat, low-fat, or defatted. Full-fat flour is the most widely available for use in home baking. Because of its strong nutty flavor, it is often used with other flours or in recipes with spices, nuts, or chocolate to mask its taste. Soy flour is used in baked goods for its high protein and ability to retard staling.

Corn Flour. The finest flour from the milling of corn endosperm. The larger particles of milled corn, in descending order of size, are segregated for cornflakes, grits, coarse cornmeal, and fine cornmeal.

Oat Flour. The fine flour resulting from the dehulling of the oat grain prior to the rolling of the oat groats. This flour contains no gluten and is used in place of rolled oats (oatmeal) in baked goods. The addition of oat flour to home-baked products is used to maintain freshness longer, since oats contain a strong natural antioxidant.

Rice Flour. Milled from broken kernels of white or brown rice, it contains no gluten. Rice flour imparts a slightly grainy texture to baked goods. Since it is essentially tasteless, it can be used in many types of baked goods, especially those with strongly flavored flours, like soy or rye.

Amaranth Flour. Amaranth is an ancient South American low gluten grain that has been rediscovered by American consumers only within the past decade or so. It is higher in protein than corn or beans, higher in fiber than wheat, rice, soybeans, or corn, the highest in iron of the cereal grains, and rich in vitamins. It also contains the essential amino acid lysine, which is absent in most other cereal grains. The flour is milled from the whole grain. A blend of amaranth and whole wheat is reported to rival meat or eggs as a complete protein source.

Quinoa Flour. Quinoa (KEEN-wah) is another recent rediscovery of ancient South American origin. Like amaranth, it contains the essential amino acid lysine and is high in protein and iron. Unlike amaranth, it is not a grain but the fruit of an herb. Quinoa flour is milled from the whole "grain" and is very low in gluten.

Buckwheat Flour. Buckwheat is a cereal grass, not a grain, and resembles wheat in name only. It contains twice the B vitamins of wheat and is best known for its use in pancakes. The dark flour is milled from the unhulled groat, while the light flour is milled from the hulled groat and has a more delicate flavor.

Millet Flour. Ground from the whole hulled grain, it contains no gluten. Millet is considered one of the most nutritious grains and is sometimes recommended in diets for people with ulcers or colitis owing to its alkaline nature.

Teff Flour. A newcomer to the United States via its ancient roots in Africa, teff boasts higher iron than wheat, rice, millet, or oats. The flour is milled from the whole grain, which can be either white, red, or brown. The white variety imparts the mildest flavor.

Because nonwheat flours contain little or no gluten, they are most successfully used in baking soda–leavened rather than yeast-leavened recipes. For those interested in exploring the nutritional or culinary possibilities of substituting the more common nonwheat flours in whole or part for wheat flour in recipes, the following table can be used as a guide.

SUBSTITUTES FOR 1 CUP OF WHEAT FLOUR IN BAKED PRODUCTS

Rye Flour	1¼ cups
Oat Flour	1⅓ cups
Corn Flour	1 cup

Soy Flour	1½ cups
Barley Flour	1⅓ cups
Rice Flour	1 cup minus 2 tablespoons

Combinations of flours tend to produce better results. For example, a mixture of 1 cup minus 2 tablespoons of rice flour and 1¼ cups of rye flour will substitute for 2 cups of wheat flour. The bland flavor of the rice flour minimizes the strong rye taste, while the rye flour minimizes the grainy texture produced by the rice flour.

LEAVENING AGENTS

Leavening is simply the act of introducing gas bubbles into a dough or batter so that it expands. The three basic approaches to leavening are generation of carbon dioxide by the reaction of baking soda with an acid, generation of carbon dioxide by fermentation of yeast, and mechanical incorporation of air by whipping or beating. A general rule of thumb is that soda leavens batters while yeast leavens dough. There are, of course, exceptions. Yeast produces carbon dioxide slowly so it requires a strong and elastic matrix to contain the generated gas. A stiff, gluten-containing dough is needed. Batters and weak doughs are not suited to yeast leavening because they can't trap the slowly released carbon dioxide. Most of the gas would exit the mixture as it was produced. This type of mixture needs a fast-acting gas source, one that will aerate the batter or dough quickly, but not so quickly that it will collapse during baking once the leavening period is over. In the past century and a half, no more suitable product than baking soda has been found. Baking soda can liberate carbon dioxide at a controlled rate; it is inexpensive, highly purified, and nontoxic.

BAKING SODA

The combination of baking soda with an acid liberates carbon dioxide, which causes the batter or dough to expand. Baking soda is often used in recipes with naturally acid ingredients like sour milk, buttermilk, yogurt, molasses, chocolate, and fruit preserves. The following combinations can serve as a guide to the use of baking soda with some common, naturally acidic ingredients; each can be used in place of two teaspoons of commercial baking powder.

- ½ teaspoon baking soda per cup of buttermilk

- ½ teaspoon baking soda per cup of milk that has been soured with 1 tablespoon of white vinegar or lemon juice

- ½ teaspoon baking soda per cup of milk that has been soured with 1¾ teaspoons of cream of tartar

- ½ teaspoon baking soda per cup of molasses

- ½ teaspoon baking soda per 1¼ teaspoons of cream of tartar

A host of baking acids are used with baking soda in household baking powders and in the food industry. The first commercial baking powders were blends of baking soda with cream of tartar. This combination reacts very quickly so that a batter had to be mixed and put into the oven before the gas evolution was spent. This was succeeded by today's "double acting" baking powder using monocalcium phosphate instead of cream of tartar. The phosphate reacts more slowly with baking soda so that about two-thirds of the carbon dioxide is liberated during mixing of the batter and the rest only in the heat of the oven. Another of the baking powders sold today for home use contains both monocalcium phosphate and sodium aluminum sulfate. This powder releases about one-third of its carbon dioxide during mixing and two-thirds during baking.

Many home bakers prefer using baking soda with cream of tartar or one of the acidic foods instead of using a commercial baking powder. Some use baking soda together with baking powder in certain recipes. This might seem redundant, but the added baking soda provides quicker and greater leavening action than occurs with the baking powder alone. The extra baking soda also improves surface browning and flavor development since the distinctive flavors of many baked goods are formed in the outer surfaces and diffuse inward on cooling.

Producers of commercial baked goods and baking mixes have a wide choice among the baking acids. The particular combinations with baking soda are chosen based on considerable research into their effects on the finished product. The soda and acid combination does not only produce carbon dioxide; it determines the final texture of the food and indirectly affects its flavor, moisture, and general palatability. For example, sodium aluminum phosphate is used as the acid in consumer cake mixes because it has a great tolerance to variations in mixing time, amount of liquid, and oven temperature. This makes for a decent cake, no matter how inexperienced the baker. Refrigerated tubed biscuit, muffin, and roll doughs require the slow, controlled leavening obtained with the use of sodium acid pyrophosphate as the baking acid. Otherwise, they would pop their tubes. Glucono delta-lactone is used as the acid in some tubed pizza and bread doughs because its reaction with baking soda provides results more closely resembling yeast leavening.

YEAST

Yeast for baking is available in two forms, yeast cake and active dry yeast. Yeast cake, or compressed yeast, is approximately 70 percent water versus less than 10 percent water in active dry yeast. Yeast cake is the more perishable of the two but slightly more active in doughs. The principal source of yeast for baking is the brewing industry, although the brewer's yeast sold in grocery and health food stores is not active and provides nutritional rather than leavening benefits.

Yeast feeds on sugars and produces carbon dioxide and alcohol, among other by-products that together give the distinctively characteristic flavor of a yeast-leavened product. Adding limited amounts of sugar to a dough will increase yeast activity. Too much sugar dehydrates the yeast cells and reduces their activity. This is why sweet breads usually require extra yeast and why cookie and cake batters are inappropriate for yeast. Excess salt has the same inhibiting effect as excess sugar.

Yeast fermentation produces small amounts of acids, so that as much as ¼ teaspoon of baking soda per cup of flour can be added to accelerate the rising of yeast-leavened breads. This can be tricky since enough fermentation must occur to neutralize all the baking soda. An alternative approach is to grow active dry yeast in acidic fruit juice overnight. This can then be used in a dough or batter with the baking soda. Thin batters can be baked immediately. Thick batters or doughs can be left to rise in a warm spot for up to a half hour before baking.

Sourdoughs are a product of fermentation by natural yeasts and lactobacillus bacteria from the air. These bacteria produce the acids that account for sourdough's distinctive taste. The airborne yeast works much better in this acidic dough than commercial yeast. The strains of yeast and bacteria native to different parts of the United States make the taste of sourdough breads unique in different regions. San Francisco sourdough is irreproducible elsewhere because its bacteria is unique to the Bay Area. Likewise, a sourdough starter transplanted from San Francisco will eventually be changed by the bacteria native to its new home.

AIR

Prior to soda leavening, thin batters, as for pancakes and waffles, and raised cakes were aerated mechanically. In its simplest form this involved tediously whipping air into the batter and then cooking before all the air could escape. Beaten eggs and especially well-beaten egg whites can retain a fair amount of air bubbles and were often used. Adding creamed butter and sugar, whipped to a light texture, was also a common way to incorporate air into a cake batter.

Mechanical leavening is still used in preparing batters today, but as a complement to soda leavening. Vegetable shortenings have replaced butter because they can incorporate more air and form smaller air pockets. Electric mixers have replaced hand beating and whipping to produce the smallest and most uniformly distributed air pockets. The carbon dioxide liberated from the baking soda reaction then expands the air pockets and completes the leavening.

OTHER INGREDIENTS

While flour and leavening form the foundation, the amount of water, and a limited number of other ingredients determines the particular character of most baked goods, differentiating the breads from the biscuits, the rolls from the cakes, the crumbs from the flakes.

SHORTENING

The term "shortening" was coined in the early nineteenth century for oils or fats added to baked goods. These were supposed to "shorten" or break up the gluten to give the product a more tender crumb. The behavior of fats and oils in baking is actually more complicated, depending on the particular type and the amount used.

The liquid shortenings used today are vegetable oils—corn, safflower, sunflower, olive, and canola. Oils are used in small amounts to add moistness and tenderness to cakes, waffles, pancakes, breads, and in any batter product that cooks to a crumb texture. The most widely used solid shortenings are based on hydrogenated vegetable oils. The hydrogenation process raises the melting point of the oil to above room temperature and produces the optimal fat crystal size to readily incorporate large amounts of air on subsequent whipping. Commercial solid shortenings, like Crisco, are hydrogenated vegetable oil that has already been whipped to incorporate very fine air bubbles. The alternative to this type of shortening is hand-creamed butter or margarine.

Pastry calls for solid shortening so that alternate layers of dough and fat will produce the desired flakiness. Use of chilled utensils and surfaces is usually recommended for preparation of pastry doughs to avoid melting of the shortening and losing flakiness. Solid shortenings are used in cakes not to promote flakiness, but to provide a more moist and tender crumb. This can be achieved with oil alone, but the solid shortening provides leavening as well from the fine air bubbles it brings to the batter.

Shortening is also used in some bread doughs, but for a function contrary to its name. Small amounts of oil or fat do add to moistness and tenderness, as in cakes, but they also promote greater loaf volume.

EGGS

Eggs are used in batters mainly for their protein and fat contributions. On heating, egg protein coagulates into films or filaments that help retain the leavening gases and form an open cell or crumb structure. The egg fats serve as shortening. Beaten egg whites will hold large amounts of air and are often used with creamed butter or margarine or commercial shortening to leaven cakes.

MILK

Milk provides water and, like eggs, protein and fat that contribute to crumb structure and tenderness. It also accelerates surface browning. Milk must be scalded and cooled prior to use in yeast-leavened products to alter milk serum proteins that would otherwise interact with flour proteins and produce a slack and sticky dough.

SUGAR

Sugar (and its functional, nutritional, and caloric equivalents, honey, molasses, corn syrup, brown sugar, and malt syrup) is used principally as a sweetener in batters and doughs, and a promoter of surface browning. In moderate amounts, sugar is a nutrient for yeast, while at high levels it inhibits fermentation. Sugar is also hygroscopic (it attracts water) and retards gluten development by competing with the flour for available water. That is why yeast-raised sweet doughs take longer to develop, while after baking they yield moist and tender products that stay fresh longer. The sugar holds onto water and retards staling.

SALT

Salt is used in most batters and doughs for taste. In bread doughs, excess salt slows yeast activity and makes the gluten less elastic. Compact, dense loaves result. At normal levels, salt keeps the protein-digesting enzymes in the flour from destroying the gluten.

THE BAKING PROCESS

For leavened products like breads, biscuits, quick breads, rolls, muffins, pancakes, scones, and waffles, the baking process balances the growth of entrapped gas bubbles with the change in gluten structure from stretched to set.

In yeast-leavened doughs, most of the structure is established during raising. In the oven, the dough goes through a rapid additional expansion (oven spring) because of the growth of gas bubbles from a combination of steam, increased yeast activity, and the natural expansion of gases at high temperatures. The heat, however, soon kills the yeast and stops fermentation. The flour's starch gels in the hot dough and sets the gluten structure. This process proceeds from the outside of the loaf inward so that loaf size is established early in baking. Once the crumb at the center of the loaf is set, further baking lowers the moisture content of the bread and browns the crust.

In soda-leavened batters, the leavening gas (carbon dioxide) is generated much too quickly for the gluten to develop and contain it. These batters must be mixed just before baking. In the hot oven, it becomes a contest between the gas bubbles trying to escape and the batter trying to form a crumb structure to hold them in. Since there is no gluten to set this structure, it is formed by the combination of proteins from all sources, usually the flours, eggs, and milk. Thin batters, as for pancakes, need high heat and short cooking times to trap the leavening gases and produce a light, airy texture. Thicker batters, as for quick breads and muffins, will hold the leavening gases longer, so they can be baked at lower temperatures for longer times. This lets the middle bake thoroughly without burning the outside.

For most baked goods, staling is not the simple loss of moisture it appears to be. During baking, water is released from the flour proteins and absorbed by its starch, which forms a gel. This is what happens when you use flour to thicken a sauce. Below the gelatinization temperature of the starch (about 140 degrees), the sauce is thin. At this temperature, the sauce suddenly thickens as the starch absorbs water and forms a gel. A bread, cake, or cookie fresh from the oven is soft because its starch is still gelled. On cooling, the starch loses some water and hardens again. Most of this water is lost through the crust as steam. This is why freshly baked bread should not cool in its pan. The trapped steam will make the crust soggy.

A small amount of starch stays gelled even after cooling and only slowly releases water to the crust. The crust absorbs this water in its dried-out starch and protein. This turns bread crust from dry and crisp to tough and leathery; a cookie or cracker turns from crisp to soft. Left uncovered, the baked good will eventually lose all of its moisture and become permanently stale. Well-wrapped goods will also stale, but they can be temporarily refreshed because they still have enough trapped moisture. Wrapping tightly and reheating lets the starch absorb this moisture and gel again. This works well for breads, reviving a fresh texture, at least while it is still warm.

It is a peculiarity of the starch in flour that when its

hot gel cools to room temperature and then to freezing, its water holding capacity is at a minimum just before the freezing point. That is why, contrary to intuition, fresh bread will actually stale more quickly when stored wrapped in the refrigerator than when kept well wrapped at room temperature. This is also why it is best to freeze homemade baked goods that will not be served within a few days. Commercially baked goods and home-baked goods from prepared mixes stay fresh longer whether refrigerated or not because most contain emulsifiers to control the movement and loss of moisture over time.

The following section combines the above techniques and ingredients, plus some delicious additions, to provide a sampling of recipes demonstrating the use of baking soda. Most of these recipes use all-purpose flour, but you are encouraged to experiment with flour blends to develop your own unique variations. As you bake and sample each creation, you can reflect on the physical and chemical processes that conspired to such pleasing ends. Better yet, just enjoy.

QUICK BREADS AND MUFFINS

In the following recipes, I call for cultured buttermilk powder (we use Saco) instead of fresh buttermilk, but not just for convenience. You can vary the intensity of buttermilk flavor or adjust to changes in the amount of baking soda used by adding more or less buttermilk powder without changing the amount of liquid. Where margarine is listed in any recipe in this section or the others (Cookies, Breakfast, Desserts), I have used a vegetable oil or corn oil stick margarine. Butter is an acceptable substitute. Tub margarines and "light" margarines will not work as well because they contain less oil and more water.

DATE-NUT BREAD
Serves 10 to 12

2½ cups all-purpose flour
1¼ teaspoons baking soda
½ cup light brown sugar
1 teaspoon salt
1 cup chopped dates
¾ cup chopped walnuts
¾ cup milk
5 tablespoons white vinegar
¼ cup solid vegetable shortening, melted
2 large eggs, beaten

1. Preheat the oven to 350 degrees. Grease a 9 × 5 × 2½-inch loaf pan.

2. Combine the flour, baking soda, brown sugar, and salt. Stir in the dates and walnuts. In a separate bowl, blend the milk, vinegar, melted shortening, and eggs. Stir the liquid into the dry ingredients and mix only until smooth. Turn into the pan. Bake for about 60 minutes, or until a cake tester inserted in the center comes out clean. Cool in the pan for 10 minutes, then transfer to a rack. Serve at room temperature.

APPLE-NUT MUFFINS
Makes 6 4-inch muffins

1½ cups all-purpose flour
½ cup quick-cooking oats
⅔ cup light brown sugar
1 teaspoon baking soda
2 teaspoons cream of tartar
1 teaspoon ground cinnamon
½ teaspoon salt
¼ teaspoon grated nutmeg
1 cup peeled and coarsely chopped apple
½ cup chopped walnuts
½ cup raisins
¼ cup cold milk
½ cup (1 stick) margarine, just melted
2 large eggs, beaten

1. Preheat the oven to 400 degrees. Lightly grease 6 4-inch muffin cups.

2. Combine the dry ingredients, then mix in the apple, walnuts, and raisins. In a separate bowl, blend the milk, melted margarine, and eggs. Stir the liquid mixture into the dry ingredients and mix only until moistened. Fill the muffin cups about ⅔ full. Bake for about 15 minutes, or until a cake tester inserted in the center of a muffin comes out clean. Serve warm or cool in the pan for 10 minutes, then transfer to a rack and serve at room temperature.

OLD-FASHIONED CORN BREAD
Serves 8 to 10

1 cup all-purpose flour
1½ cups yellow cornmeal
½ cup cultured buttermilk powder
¾ teaspoon baking soda
1 teaspoon salt
2 large eggs, beaten
1½ cups water
3 tablespoons solid vegetable shortening, melted

1. Preheat the oven to 425 degrees. Grease an 8-inch square pan.

2. Combine the dry ingredients. In a separate bowl, beat the eggs, water, and melted shortening with an electric mixer. Add the liquid ingredients to the dry, stirring only until smooth. Turn into the pan. Bake for about 25 minutes, or until a cake tester inserted in the center comes out clean. Serve hot.

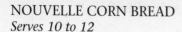

NOUVELLE CORN BREAD
Serves 10 to 12

2½ cups all-purpose flour
1 cup yellow cornmeal
2 teaspoons baking soda
1 teaspoon salt
¾ cup shredded whole milk mozzarella cheese
1½ cups milk
⅓ cup balsamic vinegar
⅓ cup olive oil
2 large eggs, beaten

1. Preheat the oven to 350 degrees. Grease a 9 × 5 × 2½-inch loaf pan.

2. Combine the dry ingredients, then blend in the mozzarella. In a separate bowl, stir together the milk, vinegar, oil, and eggs. Add the liquid to the dry blend, stirring only until smooth. Turn into the pan. Bake for about 45 minutes, or until a cake tester inserted in the center comes out clean. Cool in the pan for 10 minutes, then transfer to a rack. Serve at room temperature.

BUTTERMILK AMARANTH/CORN BREAD
Serves 10 to 12

2½ cups all-purpose flour
1½ cups amaranth flour or yellow cornmeal
¾ cup cultured buttermilk powder
⅓ cup sugar
2 teaspoons baking soda
½ cup corn oil
2 cups water
2 large eggs, beaten

1. Preheat the oven to 350 degrees. Grease a 9 × 5 × 2½-inch loaf pan.

2. Combine the dry ingredients. Add the oil and water to the eggs. Stir the liquid into the dry ingredients and mix only until smooth. Turn into the pan. Bake for about 60 minutes, or until a cake tester inserted in the center comes out clean. Cool in the pan for 10 minutes, then transfer to a rack. Serve at room temperature.

PUMPKIN BREAD
Serves 10 to 12

3 cups all-purpose flour
1 cup sugar
2 teaspoons baking soda
2 teaspoons ground cinnamon
1 teaspoon grated nutmeg
½ teaspoon salt
¼ teaspoon cream of tartar
1 cup raisins
1 cup chopped roasted cashews
3 large eggs, beaten
1½ cups canned pumpkin filling
¼ cup corn oil
1 cup water

1. Preheat the oven to 350 degrees. Grease a 9 × 5 × 2½-inch loaf pan.

2. Combine the dry ingredients, then blend in the raisins and cashews. In a separate bowl, beat the eggs, pumpkin, and oil with an electric mixer. Add the water and whip briefly. Stir the liquid into the dry blend and mix only until smooth. Turn into the pan. Bake for about 75 minutes, or until a cake tester inserted in the center comes out clean. Cool in the pan for 10 minutes, then transfer to a rack. Serve at room temperature.

HARVEST BREAD
Serves 10 to 12

The ketchup is a convenient source of tomato, vinegar, and sugar.

2½ cups all-purpose flour
½ cup yellow cornmeal
½ cup quick-cooking oats
1 cup light brown sugar
2 teaspoons baking soda
2 teaspoons ground cinnamon
1 cup raisins
2 large eggs, beaten
½ cup canned pumpkin filling
½ cup tomato ketchup
¼ cup corn oil
1½ cups apple juice

1. Preheat the oven to 350 degrees. Grease a 9 × 5 × 2½-inch loaf pan.

2. Combine the dry ingredients, then stir in the raisins. In a separate bowl, beat the eggs, pumpkin, ketchup, and oil with an electric mixer. Add the apple juice and whip briefly. Stir the liquid into the dry blend and mix only until smooth. Turn into the pan. Bake for about 75 minutes, or until a cake tester inserted in the center comes out clean. Cool in the pan for 10 minutes, then transfer to a rack. Serve at room temperature.

EGGPLANT/ZUCCHINI BREAD
Serves 10 to 12

2 cups all-purpose flour
1½ cups sugar
2¼ teaspoons baking soda
1 tablespoon ground cinnamon
1 teaspoon grated nutmeg
¼ teaspoon cream of tartar
1 cup raisins
2 cups coarsely grated peeled eggplant (not too wet or seedy)
    or zucchini
1 cup corn oil
2 teaspoons vanilla extract
3 large eggs, beaten

1. Preheat the oven to 375 degrees. Grease a 9 × 5 × 2½-inch loaf pan.

2. Combine the dry ingredients, then stir in the raisins and eggplant or zucchini. Put the beaten eggs in a separate bowl and add the oil and vanilla. Add the liquid to the dry blend, stirring only until smooth. Turn into the pan. Bake for about 70 minutes, or until a cake tester inserted in the center comes out clean. Cool in the pan for 10 minutes, then transfer to a rack. Serve at room temperature.

ZUCCHINI MUFFINS
Makes 6 4-inch muffins

2 cups all-purpose flour
¾ cup sugar
¾ teaspoon baking soda
¾ teaspoon baking powder
¾ teaspoon salt
1 teaspoon ground cinnamon
1 teaspoon grated nutmeg
1 cup coarsely grated zucchini
½ cup raisins
½ cup chopped walnuts
¾ cup corn oil
2 teaspoons vanilla extract
3 large eggs, beaten

1. Preheat the oven to 375 degrees. Grease 6 4-inch muffin cups.

2. Combine the dry ingredients, then stir in the zucchini, raisins, and walnuts. In a separate bowl, blend the oil, vanilla, and eggs. Stir the liquid into the dry ingredients and mix only until smooth. Fill the muffin cups ⅔ full. Bake for about 25 minutes or until a cake tester inserted in the center of a muffin comes out clean. Serve warm or let cool in the cups for 10 minutes, then transfer to a rack and serve at room temperature.

SIMPLE SODA BREAD
Serves 8 to 12

4 cups sifted all-purpose flour
½ cup cultured buttermilk powder
1 tablespoon sugar
2 teaspoons baking soda
1 teaspoon salt
1 cup raisins
1½ cups cold water
⅓ cup olive oil

1. Preheat the oven to 350 degrees. Grease a baking sheet.

2. Combine the dry ingredients, then stir in the raisins. Add the water and stir to a soft dough. Knead in the oil. Turn onto a lightly floured surface and knead to form a smooth ball. Pat by hand on the baking sheet to about a 1½-inch thickness. With a sharp knife score into 4 sections. Bake 45 minutes, or until the bread is browned and a cake tester inserted in the center comes out clean. Serve warm with butter.

BROWN BREAD MUFFINS
Makes 6 4-inch muffins

2 cups whole wheat flour
⅔ cup all-purpose flour
⅔ cup light brown sugar
2 teaspoons baking soda
⅔ cup cultured buttermilk powder
1 teaspoon grated nutmeg
¾ cup raisins
2 cups water

1. Preheat the oven to 350 degrees. Grease 6 4-inch muffin cups.

2. Combine the dry ingredients, then stir in the raisins. Stir in the water and mix only until smooth. Fill the muffin cups about ⅔ full. Bake for about 35 minutes or until a cake tester inserted in the center comes out clean. Serve warm or let cool in the cups for 10 minutes, then transfer to a rack and serve at room temperature.

BANANA-OAT-RAISIN MUFFINS
Makes a dozen 2½-inch muffins

1½ cups quick-cooking oats
½ cup all-purpose flour
½ cup whole wheat flour
1 teaspoon baking soda
1 teaspoon baking powder
½ teaspoon salt
1 cup raisins
1 cup milk
1 cup pureed ripe banana
¼ cup corn oil
2 teaspoons vanilla extract
1 large egg, beaten

1. Preheat the oven to 400 degrees. Grease 12 2½-inch muffin cups.

2. Combine the dry ingredients, then mix in the raisins. In a separate bowl, blend the milk, banana, oil, vanilla, and egg. Stir the liquid mixture into the dry ingredients and mix only until moistened. Fill the muffin cups. Bake for about 20 minutes, or until a cake tester inserted in the center of a muffin comes out clean. Serve warm or let cool in the cups for 10 minutes, then transfer to a rack and serve at room temperature.

COOKIES

BIG AND EASY OATMEAL COOKIES
Makes 1½ to 2 dozen

3 cups quick-cooking oats
1 cup all-purpose flour
1½ cups light brown sugar
1 teaspoon baking soda
1 cup raisins
¼ cup cold water
2 teaspoons vanilla extract
¾ cup (1½ sticks) margarine, just melted
1 large cold egg, beaten

1. Preheat the oven to 350 degrees. Lightly grease 2 cookie sheets.

2. Combine the dry ingredients, then stir in the raisins. In a separate bowl, blend the cold water, vanilla, melted margarine, and egg. Stir the liquid into the dry mixture only until evenly moistened. Shape with floured hands into 1½-inch balls and place 2 inches apart on the cookie sheets. Bake for 18 to 20 minutes, or until lightly browned. Cool on the cookie sheets for 3 minutes, then transfer to a rack and serve at room temperature.

BIRTHDAY COOKIE
Serves 10 to 12
Everyone will love this alternative to birthday cake.

1½ cups all-purpose flour
¾ cup light brown sugar
1 teaspoon baking soda
½ teaspoon salt
1½ cups semisweet chocolate morsels
¼ cup corn syrup
2 teaspoons vanilla extract
½ cup (1 stick) margarine, just melted
1 large cold egg, beaten

1. Combine the dry ingredients, then stir in the morsels. In a separate bowl, blend the syrup, vanilla, melted margarine, and egg. Stir the liquid into the dry mixture only until evenly moistened. Refrigerate, covered, for at least 1 hour.

2. Preheat the oven to 325 degrees. Grease a round 12-inch foil baking pan; spread the dough to within 1½ inches of its edge. Spell out a birthday greeting with additional morsels lightly pressed in the surface. Place the pan on a cookie sheet and bake for about 30 minutes, or until the edges are firm. Place the foil pan on a rack and cool to room temperature.

CHOCOLATE CHIP REDUX

Makes 3 to 4 dozen

Mayonnaise is a blend of oil, egg, and vinegar—a convenient source of shortening, protein, and baking acid.

3¾ cups all-purpose flour
2 cups light brown sugar
2½ teaspoons baking soda
¾ teaspoon salt
2 cups semisweet chocolate morsels
¾ cup (1½ sticks) margarine, just melted
1½ cups mayonnaise

1. Preheat the oven to 350 degrees. Lightly grease 2 cookie sheets.

2. Combine the dry ingredients, then stir in the morsels. In a separate bowl, whip the melted margarine into the mayonnaise with an electric mixer, then add this to the dry mixture. Beat briefly to a coarse dough. Shape into 1½-inch balls and place 2 inches apart on the cookie sheets. Bake for about 15 minutes, or until lightly browned. Cool on the cookie sheets for 3 minutes, then transfer to a rack and serve at room temperature.

ORANGE-APRICOT COOKIES
Makes 3 to 4 dozen

1 cup all-purpose flour
¾ cup whole wheat flour
¼ cup sugar
½ teaspoon baking soda
½ teaspoon ground cinnamon
¼ teaspoon salt
¾ cup chopped dried apricots
1 teaspoon grated orange zest
½ cup fresh orange juice
¼ cup corn oil
1 large egg, beaten

1. Preheat the oven to 375 degrees.

2. Combine the dry ingredients, then stir in the chopped apricots and orange zest. In a separate bowl, blend the orange juice, oil, and egg. Add the liquid mixture to the dry ingredients and mix until uniform. Drop by tablespoonfuls about 1 inch apart onto ungreased cookie sheets. Bake for about 10 minutes, or until lightly browned. Cool on the cookie sheets for 3 minutes, then transfer to a rack and serve at room temperature.

PEANUT BUTTER-CHOCOLATE COOKIES
Makes 3 to 4 dozen

¾ *cup sugar*
11 *tablespoons margarine, softened*
2 *large eggs, beaten*
1 *teaspoon vanilla extract*
6 *ounces semisweet chocolate, melted*
2 *cups quick-cooking oats*
1½ *cups all-purpose flour*
1 *teaspoon baking soda*
2 *cups peanut butter chips*

1. With an electric mixer, cream the sugar and margarine. Add the eggs and vanilla and beat until smooth. Add the melted chocolate and beat until smooth. In a separate bowl, blend the oats, flour, and baking soda. Gradually beat this dry blend into the liquid mixture. Mix only until uniformly moistened. Mix in the peanut butter chips. Refrigerate, covered, for at least 1 hour.

2. Preheat the oven to 350 degrees. Lightly grease 2 cookie sheets. Shape the dough into 1½-inch balls and place 2 inches apart on the cookie sheets. Bake for about 15 minutes, or until lightly browned. Cool on the cookie sheets for 3 minutes, then transfer to a rack and serve at room temperature.

CHOCOLATE-PEANUT BUTTER COOKIES
Makes 2 to 3 dozen

1½ cups light brown sugar
1 cup (2 sticks) margarine, softened
2 cups chunky peanut butter
2 large eggs, beaten
2 teaspoons butter extract
2 cups all-purpose flour
2 teaspoons baking soda
¼ teaspoon salt
2 cups semisweet chocolate morsels

1. With an electric mixer, cream the brown sugar, margarine, and peanut butter. Add the eggs and extract and beat until smooth. In a separate bowl, blend the flour, baking soda, and salt. Gradually beat this dry blend into the liquid mixture. Mix only until uniformly moistened. Mix in the morsels. Refrigerate, covered, for at least 1 hour.

2. Preheat the oven to 375 degrees. Lightly grease 2 cookie sheets. Shape the dough into 1½-inch balls and place 2 inches apart on the cookie sheets. Bake for about 15 minutes, or until lightly browned. Cool on the cookie sheets for 3 minutes, then transfer to a rack and serve at room temperature.

BRAN-APPLE BARS
Makes 8 to 10 bars

1 cup whole bran cereal
½ cup skim milk
1 cup all-purpose flour
½ teaspoon baking soda
½ teaspoon ground cinnamon
¼ teaspoon grated nutmeg
5 tablespoons margarine, softened
½ cup light brown sugar
2 large egg whites
1 cup peeled and finely chopped apple

1. Preheat the oven to 350 degrees. Lightly grease a 9-inch square baking pan.

2. Soak the bran cereal in the milk until the milk is absorbed. In a small bowl, blend the dry ingredients. In a medium-size bowl, cream the margarine and brown sugar with an electric mixer; add the egg whites and beat well. Add the dry ingredients and mix until just smooth. Stir in the bran mixture and apple. Pour into the baking pan. Bake 30 minutes, or until a cake tester inserted in the center comes out clean. Cool in the pan on a rack to room temperature.

BREAKFAST

ORANGE-RAISIN SCONES
Makes about 2 dozen

3 cups all-purpose flour
½ cup sugar
2 teaspoons baking soda
½ cup (1 stick) cold margarine, sliced
1 cup raisins
½ cup orange juice
1 large cold egg, beaten

1. Preheat the oven to 350 degrees. Lightly grease 2 baking sheets.

2. Combine the flour, sugar, and baking soda. With an electric mixer, cut in the margarine until the mixture resembles coarse meal. Stir in the raisins. In a separate bowl, blend the orange juice into the egg. Add the liquid mixture to the dry ingredients and mix until uniform. Gather the dough into a ball. Roll the dough to a ½-inch thickness on a lightly floured surface. Cut into 3-inch circles and place them on the baking sheets about ½ inch apart. Bake for about 15 minutes, or until just browned. Serve warm.

GRAHAM BUTTERMILK PANCAKES
Makes 20 to 24 4-inch pancakes

2 cups all-purpose flour
½ cup finely crushed graham crackers (3 whole crackers)
½ cup cultured buttermilk powder
2 tablespoons sugar
2 teaspoons baking soda
½ teaspoon salt
4 tablespoons corn oil
2 teaspoons vanilla extract
2 cups water
2 large eggs, beaten

1. Combine the dry ingredients. In a separate bowl, mix the oil, vanilla, water, and eggs. Stir the liquid into the dry ingredients only until smooth. Pour enough batter to make a 4-inch-wide pancake onto a hot, lightly greased griddle. Cook until bubbles rise to the top and the underside is lightly browned. Flip and brown on the other side. Repeat with the rest of the batter.

CORNMEAL PANCAKES
Makes 20 to 24 4-inch pancakes

1 cup all-purpose flour
1 cup yellow cornmeal
⅓ cup instant nonfat milk powder
2 tablespoons sugar
2½ teaspoons baking soda
½ teaspoon cream of tartar
½ teaspoon salt
1 cup water
3 tablespoons margarine, melted
3 large eggs, beaten

1. Combine the dry ingredients. In a separate bowl, mix the water, melted margarine, and eggs. Stir the liquid into the dry ingredients only until smooth. Pour the batter onto a hot, lightly greased griddle. Cook until bubbles rise to the top and the underside is lightly browned. Flip and brown on the other side.

WAFFLES
Makes 16 to 20

2 cups all-purpose flour
½ teaspoon baking soda
½ teaspoon salt
4 large eggs
¼ cup sugar
2 cups plain yogurt or sour cream

1. Preheat a waffle iron.

2. Combine the flour, baking soda, and salt. In a separate bowl, beat the eggs and sugar with an electric mixer until thickened. Fold in the dry mixture and the yogurt or sour cream alternately, beginning and ending with the dry mixture. Blend just until uniform. Prepare the waffles according to the waffle iron manufacturer's instructions.

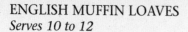

ENGLISH MUFFIN LOAVES
Serves 10 to 12

Cornmeal, for sprinkling
6 cups all-purpose flour
2 packages active dry quick-rising yeast
1 tablespoon sugar
2 teaspoons salt
¼ teaspoon baking soda
2½ cups low-fat milk

1. Grease 2 8½ × 4½-inch pans and sprinkle them with cornmeal.

2. Combine 3 cups of the flour with the yeast, sugar, salt, and baking soda. In a saucepan, heat the milk until very warm (120 to 130 degrees). Do not boil. Add to the dry mixture and beat well. Stir in the remaining flour to make a stiff batter. Spoon into the pans. Cover; let rise in a warm area for 45 minutes.

3. Preheat the oven to 400 degrees. Bake the loaves for 25 minutes. Remove the loaves from the pans immediately and cool on a rack to room temperature.

FUNNEL CAKES
Serves 10 to 12

Oil, for frying
1¼ cups all-purpose flour
2 tablespoons granulated sugar
1 teaspoon baking soda
¾ teaspoon baking powder
¼ teaspoon salt
1 large egg, beaten
¾ cup milk
Confectioners' sugar, for sprinkling

1. Heat ¼ inch of oil in a skillet. Combine the dry ingredients. In a separate bowl, blend the egg and milk. Add the dry ingredients and beat just until smooth. Using a funnel with at least a ⅜-inch opening and your finger to cover the bottom, dribble about ¼ cup of batter at a time into the center of the skillet in a slow spiral pattern. Fry 2 minutes, or until golden brown, turning once. Drain on paper towels and sprinkle with confectioners' sugar. Serve hot with pancake syrup.

DESSERTS

CRANBERRY CAKE
Serves 8 to 12

2¼ cups all-purpose flour
1½ cups quick-cooking oats
1 tablespoon baking powder
½ teaspoon baking soda
2 cups chopped cranberries
¾ cup (1½ sticks) margarine, softened
1 cup sugar
1 cup milk
3 large eggs
2 teaspoons orange extract

1. Preheat the oven to 350 degrees. Grease and flour a 10-inch tube pan.

2. Combine the dry ingredients, then stir in the cranberries. In a separate bowl, cream the margarine and sugar with an electric mixer until light and fluffy. Add the milk and eggs one at a time, beating after each addition. Stir in the extract. Add the dry ingredients and beat until uniform. Turn into the pan. Bake about 60 minutes, or until a cake tester inserted in the center comes out clean. Cool in the pan for 10 minutes, then remove and transfer to a rack for complete cooling. Serve at room temperature drizzled with Yogurt Glaze (page 135).

BANANA CHIP CAKE
Serves 8 to 10

1¼ cups sifted cake flour
¾ teaspoon baking soda
½ teaspoon salt
1 cup sugar
½ cup solid vegetable shortening
2 large eggs
¾ cup mashed banana (about 2 medium bananas)
1 cup semisweet chocolate minimorsels

1. Preheat the oven to 350 degrees. Grease and flour a 9-inch square pan.

2. Combine the flour, baking soda, and salt. Using an electric mixer in a separate bowl, gradually add the sugar to the shortening and cream until light and fluffy. Add the eggs one at a time, beating after each addition. Blend in the banana. Add the dry ingredients and chocolate morsels to the banana mixture and mix well. Turn into the pan. Bake 35 minutes, or until a cake tester inserted in the center comes out clean. Cool in the pan on a rack to room temperature.

SOUR CREAM POUND CAKE
Serves 8 to 12

3 cups all-purpose flour
½ teaspoon baking soda
¼ teaspoon salt
3 cups sugar
1 cup (2 sticks) margarine
6 large eggs
1 cup sour cream
2 teaspoons vanilla extract

1. Preheat the oven to 350. Grease and flour a 10-inch tube pan.

2. Combine the flour, baking soda, and salt. Using an electric mixer in a separate bowl, cream the margarine and sugar until light and fluffy. Add the eggs one at a time, beating after each addition. Stir in the sour cream and vanilla. Add the dry ingredients and mix well. Turn into the pan. Bake 85 minutes, or until a cake tester inserted in the center comes out clean. Cool in the pan for 10 minutes, then remove and transfer to a rack for complete cooling. Serve at room temperature.

EXTRA CHOCOLATE CAKE

Serves 8 to 12

This is a great cake made even better with Fudge Frosting (page 136).

2 cups cake flour
1 teaspoon baking soda
¾ teaspoon salt
½ cup solid vegetable shortening
1½ cups light brown sugar
2 large eggs
3 ounces unsweetened chocolate, melted
1 teaspoon vanilla extract
1 cup plus 2 tablespoons milk

1. Preheat the oven to 350 degrees. Grease and flour 2 9-inch layer cake pans.

2. Combine the dry ingredients. In a separate bowl, cream the shortening and brown sugar with an electric mixer. Beat in the eggs until the mixture is light and fluffy. Stir in the melted chocolate and vanilla. Beat in the dry mixture alternately with the milk, beginning and ending with dry ingredients. Beat until smooth and uniform. Pour the batter into the pans. Bake 25 minutes, or until a cake tester inserted in the center comes out clean. Cool in the pans for 10 minutes, then remove and transfer to racks for complete cooling. Frost and serve at room temperature.

SUPER CHOCOLATE CAKE
Serves 8 to 12

Make sure to put this one under the Fudge Frosting (page 136).

2¾ cups cake flour
1 teaspoon baking soda
¼ teaspoon salt
¾ cup (1½ sticks) margarine
6 ounces semisweet chocolate
1½ cups sugar
3 large eggs
2 teaspoons vanilla extract
1½ cups water

1. Preheat the oven to 350 degrees. Grease and flour 2 9-inch layer pans.

2. Combine the dry ingredients in a mixing bowl. In a saucepan, carefully melt the margarine and chocolate together, stirring continuously. As soon as the chocolate is completely melted, remove from the heat. Blend in the sugar. Transfer the mixture to a separate mixing bowl. With an electric mixer, beat in the eggs one at a time until smooth. Add the vanilla. Stir in ½ cup of the dry mixture. Beat in the remaining dry mixture alternately with the water until smooth and uniform. Pour into the pans. Bake 35 minutes, or until a cake tester inserted in the center comes out clean. Cool in the pans for 10 minutes, then remove and transfer to racks for complete cooling. Cool to room temperature, frost, and serve.

ALMOND POUND CAKE

Serves 8 to 12

Cover this with Chocolate Glaze (page 137), and the perfect snack cake becomes the perfect dessert cake.

2 cups all-purpose flour
¼ teaspoon baking soda
1½ teaspoons cream of tartar
1 cup sugar
7 ounces almond paste
1 cup (2 sticks) margarine
4 large eggs
½ cup milk

1. Preheat the oven to 350 degrees. Grease and flour a Bundt pan.

2. Combine the flour, baking soda, and cream of tartar. In a separate bowl, cream the sugar, almond paste, and margarine with an electric mixer. Beat in the eggs one at a time until light and fluffy. Beat in the dry mixture alternately with the milk, beginning and ending with the dry mix until uniform. Pour into the pan. Bake 70 minutes, or until a cake tester inserted in the center comes out clean. Cool in the pan for 10 minutes, then remove and transfer to a rack and cool to room temperature. Drizzle with glaze, if desired.

YOGURT GLAZE

This is the finishing touch for the Cranberry Cake (page 129) and any snack cake or quick bread.

1½ cups plain nonfat yogurt
3 tablespoons light brown sugar
2 teaspoons vanilla extract

1. Blend well until smooth.

FUDGE FROSTING

This is the perfect chocolate lovers frosting for Extra Chocolate Cake (page 132) and Super Chocolate Cake (page 133).

1 cup granulated sugar
4 tablespoons unsweetened cocoa powder
4 tablespoons unsalted butter
½ cup milk
2 tablespoons corn syrup
1 teaspoon vanilla extract
1 cup confectioners' sugar

1. Combine the sugar, cocoa, butter, milk, and syrup in a heavy saucepan. Heat to boiling, stirring occasionally. Remove from the heat. Beat in the vanilla and confectioners' sugar; continue beating until thick enough to spread.

CHOCOLATE GLAZE

When chocolate frosting is too much, but an unglazed dessert won't do, Chocolate Glaze will lightly dress up your cake.

5 tablespoons margarine
2 cups confectioners' sugar
2 teaspoons vanilla extract
2 ounces unsweetened chocolate, melted
2 tablespoons hot water

1. Melt the margarine in a saucepan over medium heat. Stir in the confectioners' sugar, vanilla, melted chocolate, and hot water until well blended. If the glaze is too thick, add additional hot water 1 tablespoon at a time until it is the desired consistency.

Anyone who has discovered a use for baking soda that is not presented here is cordially invited to send it to me c/o HarperCollins Publishers, 10 East 53rd Street, New York, NY 10022. You'll have our appreciation and the satisfaction of continuing a tradition started in your great-grandmother's time.

BIBLIOGRAPHY

American Chemical Industry: A History, William Haynes. New York: Van Nostrand, 1949.

American Food, Evan Jones. New York: Dutton, 1975.

Appleton's Cyclopaedia of American Biography, James Grant Wilson and John Fiske. New York: Appleton, 1887.

A Bibliography for Culinary Historians Using the Harvard University Libraries and the Arthur and Elizabeth Schlesinger Library of the History of Women in America, Barbara Ketcham Wheaton and Patricia M. Kelly. Cambridge, MA, 1985.

The Book of Bread, Judith and Evan Jones. New York: Harper & Row, 1982.

Carla Emery's Old Fashioned Recipe Book, Carla Emery. New York: Bantam, 1977.

The Chemistry of the Arts, Arthur L. Porter. Philadelphia: Carey & Lea, 1830.

The Complete Food Handbook, Roger P. Doyle and James L. Redding. New York: Grove Press, 1976.

A Comprehensive Treaty on Inorganic and Theoretical Chemistry, J. W. Mellor. London: Longmans, 1927.

Concise Dictionary of American Biography, 2nd ed. New York: Scribner's, 1977.

The Cook's Companion, Dorris McFerran Townsend. New York: Crown, 1978.

Dictionary of American Biography, Allen Johnson. New York: Scribner's, 1928.

The Dictionary of Medical Folklore, Carol Ann Rinzler. New York: Thomas Y. Crowell, 1979.

Dictionary of National Biography, Leslie Stephen and Sidney Lee. Oxford: Oxford University Press, 1917.

Dictionary of Scientific Biography. New York: Scribner's, 1972.

Eating in America, Waverly Root and Richard de Rochemont. New York: William Morrow, 1976.

Encyclopedia of Chemical Technology, Raymond E. Kirk and Donald F. Othmer. New York: Wiley, 1st ed., 1948; 2nd ed., 1964, 1978; 3rd ed., 1984.

English Bread & Yeast Cookery, Elizabeth David. New York: Viking, 1980.

The Food Book, James Trager. New York: Grossman, 1970.

Food in History, Reay Tannahill. New York: Stein & Day, 1973.

Foods & Nutrition Encyclopedia. Clovis, CA: Pegus Press, 1983.

Geology and World Deposits, Peter W. Harben and Robert L. Bates. London: Metal Bulletin Plc, 1990.

The Goldbecks' Guide to Good Food, Nikki and David Goldbeck. New York: New American Library, 1987.

The Grains Cookbook, Bert Greene. New York: Workman Publishing, 1988.

Great American Food Almanac, Irena Chalmers and Milton Glaser. New York: Harper & Row, 1986.

Great Oldtime Recipes, Beatriz-Maria Prada. New York: Ballantine, 1974.

A History of American Manufacturers from 1608 to 1860, J. Leander Bishop. London: Edward Young, 1868.

History of the City of New York 1609–1909, John William Leonard. New York: Journal of Commerce and Commercial Bulletin, 1910.

The Ingenious Yankees, Joseph and Frances Geis. New York: Thomas Y. Crowell, 1976.

Inventors Who Left Their Brands on America, Frank H. Olsen. New York: Bantam, 1991.

Kitchen Science, Howard Hillman. Boston: Houghton Mifflin, 1989.

Listening to America, Stuart Berg Flexner. New York: Simon and Schuster, 1982.

Made in USA, Phil Patton. New York: Grove Weidenfeld, 1992.

On Food and Cooking, Harold McGee. New York: Scribner's, 1984.

The Secret Life of Food, Martin Elkort. Los Angeles: Jeremy P. Tarcher, 1991.

Sodium Bicarbonate. Princeton, NJ: Church & Dwight, 1989.

The Supermarket Handbook, Nikki and David Goldbeck. New York: New American Library, 1976.

The Versatile Grain and the Elegant Bean, Sheryl and Mel London. New York: Simon and Schuster, 1992.

Who Was Who in America. Chicago: Marquis, 1963.

INDEX

LeBlanc, Nicolas, 4
Leg shaving aid, 65–66
Litter box deodorant, 45
Lubricant, rubber glove,
    22

Marble top stains, 45
Medicine chest uses,
    62–69
Metal cleaners, 47
Metal legs cleaner, 31
Microwave oven cleaner,
    28
Mildew remover, leather,
    44
Milk, 99
Millet flour, 91
Mouse, computer, clean-
    ing, 49–50
Mouthwash/gargle, 64
Muffins
    apple-nut, 105
    banana-oat-raisin,
        115
    brown bread, 114
    zucchini, 112
Multipurpose cleaners,
    42–43
Mummies, 56–57

Municipal water treat-
    ment, 77–78

Nail care, 66–67
Nonstick cookware
    cleaner, 27
Nouvelle corn bread, 107
Nursery presoak, 37
Nursery spotter, 37
Nursery uses, 36–39

Oat(meal)
    -banana-raisin
        muffins, 115
    cookies, big and easy,
        116
    flour, 90
Oceans, bicarbonate con-
    tent of, xiv–xv
Old-fashioned corn
    bread, 106
Orange
    -apricot cookies, 119
    -raisin scones, 123
Oven cleaner, 27–28

Paint stripping, 79–81
Pancakes
    cornmeal, 125